WHAT WILL THE CITY OF THE FUTURE LOOK LIKE?

Scenarios for the direction in which urban centers will develop over the next decades are indeed highly divergent on this question. One thing, however, can already be ascertained: urban transformation processes will require a fundamental change in thinking – from each individual, but also from us.

Urban infrastructures must become more flexible and functional in order to keep up with the requirements of growing metropolises. We at Audi are already closely examining innovative and sustainable mobility concepts that can reduce travel times and keep up with the continuing development of society. To not merely point out the problems, but to actively participate in the debate and, in doing so, play our part in driving forward solutions is a major challenge – one that we have taken on with the *Audi Urban Future Award.*

We have already laid the cornerstone for concrete mobility scenarios: at the *Audi Urban Future Award* Conference held at the Royal Institute of British Architects in London, the participating architectural firms presented their initial visions for the city of the future. We at Audi were favorably surprised that, despite their varied approaches, all of the architects see individual movement as the fundamental mobility factor of the future and have accorded the automobile an appropriate emotional status in their analysis. This gave way to many interesting discussions on possible alternatives to the existing infrastructure and systems, both at the conference and in retrospective consideration of the meeting of architects, journalists and Audi representatives. One of our goals has therefore already been achieved in this interim phase: we want to encourage an exchange of ideas and be an active participant in the discussion in order to enter into a constructive debate with critical voices and develop new concepts together with the experts in urban design. It is important to us to continue to enrich the discussion on urban mobility in the future and infuse it with new aspects.

ALISON BROOKS, ZANG KE AND RUPERT STADLER AT THE AUDI URBAN FUTURE AWARD 2010 CONFERENCE, LONDON
PHOTO: SABINE REITMAIER, © AUDI

Throughout the entire process of the competition, the continual and interdisciplinary exchange was of great importance. During a visit to the Audi facilities in Ingolstadt, the architects were able to gain a first-hand impression of how Audi deals with the subject of the future. Additionally, the architects engaged in an intensive exchange with our "Audi Think Tank", which is make up of representatives from individual disciplines such as Design, Technical Development, Brand and Corporate Strategy. I am convinced that this collaboration has broadened perspectives on both sides.

I am looking forward to the scenarios, models, visions and images on the topic of the city and mobility of tomorrow, which will be honored with an award in Venice and presented in an exhibition. For us, this is just the beginning of a far-reaching discussion of this multifaceted subject, which will continue to hold our attention in the future.

Rupert Stadler

www.audi-urban-future-award.com

ON THE ROAD TO VENICE CURATORS' PREFACE

The time has come: The future scenarios of the six architects we selected are on display in an exciting and multifaceted exhibition at the Scuola Grande della Misericordia in Venice. We have been working towards this is moment for a long time, and we have always looked forward to it with anticipation. When the award is bestowed upon the jury's selection of a vision for the city of the future and the important role that mobility will play in it, the first edition of the *Audi Urban Future Award* will come to an end.

The path we have travelled together with Audi and the architects has been long and sometimes intricate, but for us curators it was constantly stimulating and full of discoveries. Although the *Audi Urban Future Award* has the format of a competition at the end of which a winner will be declared, from the very beginning its central motivation has been cooperation rather than rivalry. The pragmatism of the automobile industry on one side, a group of utopian-minded idea givers on the other: this kind of opposition seemed to us to be not only inappropriate but, in the light of fundamental considerations, the wrong approach. Therefore, a dialogue between different spheres took its place and in the course of that dialogue ideas and perspectives, opinions and strategies were exchanged and a number of preconceptions were dismantled. Even though different languages were spoken at times in drawing a picture of the future and metaphors were employed that were not always easily comprehensible, throughout the entire process each of the participants was open and curious to learn about the concepts, desires and visions that motivated the others. Therefore, we have positioned what happened along the way to the first *Audi Urban Future Award* under the heading of "Process" and have tried to capture its essence in this publication.

Consensus among the participants, however, was not limited to the fact that mutual cooperation is the key to creating a viable picture of the future of the city and mobility. In all discussions it also became clear that mobility in a highly condensed environment – particularly in ever more rapidly growing megacities – will continue to play a central role in the future. Regardless of whether one drives a car or takes the subway, uses individual or collective means of transportation, the city is going to change just as fundamentally as will our everyday habits. And for this reason, all of the scenarios and images, models and visions that are competing for the first *Audi Urban Future Award,* and are now on display in the exhibition designed by Raumlaborberlin, are about the transformation of our reality.

It is a particular pleasure to be able to experience the culmination and conclusion of the *Audi Urban Future Award 2010* in Venice. Naturally, because the Architecture Biennale is taking place here simultaneously, in the context of which central questions of the past, present and future of architecture are being addressed from very different perspectives. But that's not the only reason. For its location, unmistakable contours and history, Venice is an unparalleled city. In the words of the writer and Nobel laureate Joseph Brodsky, who for years spent several months of every winter here, the map of the city looks like "two grilled fish sharing a plate, or perhaps like two nearly overlapping lobster claws."

The Floating City lives not only on the glamour of the early modern age, when the Venetians had gained power and influence through worldwide trade relationships. It also lives from its contemporary charm as a city without automobile traffic, yet in which the diverse effects of a global society that takes mobility for granted can still clearly be seen. Surprisingly few of these effects are noticeable when walking through Venice, which nearly amounts to a small miracle. "No matter what you set out for," noted Brodsky, "as you leave the house here, you are bound to get lost in these long, coiling lanes and passageways that beguile you to see them through, to follow them to their elusive end, which usually hits water, so that you can't even call it a cul-de-sac."

PARTICIPANTS OF THE CONFERENCE HELD AT THE ROYAL INSTITUTE OF BRITISH ARCHITECTS IN LONDON
PHOTO: SABINE REITMAIER, © AUDI

Venice is a feast for the eyes, a labyrinth full of surprises. Therein, possibly, lies a piece of the future. Because only if the eye gets its money's worth can a city be more than a conglomeration of buildings, and that will hold true in the future, as well. And so, in the middle of a labyrinth created by the past, we look with anticipation to the labyrinths of the future, through which we will navigate – presumably with the aid of digital systems. They all have one thing in common: the desire for emissions-free, low-noise, possibly driverless but above all free-flowing mobility.

Who's to say if perhaps Venice, the city of water, can be a benchmark for this utopia? In the end, what it comes down to – in the individual proposals as in the big picture – is loosening up conditions that have become all-too static and letting oneself in on an exciting future. By encouraging us to come together to consider the technological, social and aesthetic conditions that engender the future, the *Audi Urban Future Award* is taking a first step.

Sincerely,
Your Stylepark Team

www.stylepark.com

A TEMPORARY PARADISE ON THE PARADOXES OF CITY LIFE BY DEYAN SUDJIC

I first heard the term "temporary paradise syndrome" in Australia more than a decade ago. To put it simply, it reflects the tendency we have to destroy the things that we love. The term came up at one of those conferences on urban futures that, like hot spots for the transmission of avian flu, encourage those precious few notions that the world seems to have developed for dealing with the issues facing the future of the city to ricochet from continent to continent. When one city has what seems like a smart idea for addressing the ills that face it, whether it is building special bus lanes in Brazil or Colombia or culturally-led renewal and exhibitionistic architecture in Bilbao, then it's only a conference away from infecting all its competitors, who start building them too. Yet the world's major cities remain distinctively different in their essential urban DNA.

In the early 1990s, Brisbane's planners were talking to their counterparts from Seattle and Vancouver about how to deal with the way that their cities had become refuges for footloose, early adopters fleeing smog, traffic, recession and blight. For a brief moment, these cities looked like they had it all: a great natural setting, cheap housing, short commutes, clean air. These are the things that allow the relatively affluent to live in affordable, spacious suburban homes, where they can catch a glimpse of exotic wildlife as they jump into their car for the 15-minute commute to a downtown whose streets are squeaky clean and entirely free of crime. The trouble, of course, is that this is only a temporary paradise. The more people want to share it, the more that house is going to cost, the longer that commute is going to take and the more polluted the city's air is going to become.

WHAT MAKES THE CITY A CITY

The paradox of city life is that people look for it because it offers them more choices and more freedom than small towns or rural life.

A parallel phenomenon is reshaping less affluent cities. For the village dwellers of India and China, Bombay or Shanghai could also be understood as a refuge. It may involve life on the pavement or in windowless cardboard shacks, but compared with what they have left behind, such an existence offers work, money and a step up on the ladder to economic freedom. In the last analysis, cities have always acted as machines that transform the poor into the not so poor. A successful city is a place in which as many people as possible have the most choice in order to make of it what they want and need. It's a place of multiple definitions overlapping – but not necessarily interfering – with all the others. That is just as true of Brisbane and Vancouver as it is of Lagos, Bombay or Mexico City. But in order to make that possible, it's also essential that there be some shared ground rules about living together. That means shaping growth to keep alive the essential qualities of what might be called "citiness". This is a term coined by the sociologist Saskia Sassen to define that irreducible characteristic that we look for in the evolving hybrid settlements we inhabit. While they may have lost all of the urban landmarks and dense urban tissue traditionally associated with the city and the kind of social interactions that it once offered, they are all that we have left to give us the essence of what it is to be living together as humans in large groups.

DENSITY AND PERIPHERY

A new post-suburb isn't going to look like an old downtown, but if it is going to have any chance of still being a desirable place to live in ten years' time, it will have to invest in its infrastructure in the same way that cities did in the 19th century. A suburb that can't do without the car is going to be in trouble without cheap petrol. A suburb that makes no attempt to create a centre and a focus is going to have trouble offering the things that we expect of city life; even the most basic shops, cafes and education depend on us living close enough to each other to support them. And a favela or a barrio need to have the potential within them to allow their inhabitants to escape squalor and poverty, in the way that Tokyo's slums once did. That potential may have as much to do with land tenure as it does with physical or spatial qualities.

We know that a certain level of density is what makes a city work. But what we have trouble doing is persuading each other that this type of thing is worth paying for, and that we can't afford to go on relying on the farsightedness of our grandparents' generation with their massive investment in civic life. When it comes to cities, we have a way of using the tactics of the last campaign to fight the battles of the next war.

MATERIAL REALITY AND POLITICAL GEOGRAPHY

The temporary paradises of our times are not the only cities in the world to have suddenly discovered that they have been overtaken by events. In the early 2000s, London found itself going through a spurt of growth after generations of decline, which made so many of the deep-seated attitudes that the city had towards itself become out of date overnight. The city demanded a more structured approach to planning. In London, as in many cities, physical reality has overtaken political geography. In Mexico City, for example, much of the city's population doesn't live within the political boundaries of the city. It's this kind of mismatch between how we picture our cities and what is actually happening to them that accounts for some of the randomness and the accidental quality of so much development, which is more often the product of unintended consequences than of vision.

Politicians love construction cranes. They need solutions within the time frames of elections and cranes deliver them. But there are only a limited number of problems that are susceptible to this kind of time scale. The result is a constant cycle of demolition and reconstruction that is seen as a substitute for thinking about how to address the deeper issues of the city. Visions for cities tend to be the creation of boosters rather than of theorists or policy makers. City builders have always had to be pathological optimists, if not out-and-out fantasists. They belong to a tradition that connects the map makers, who parcel up packages of swamp land to sell to gullible purchasers, with the show apartment builders, who sell off plans to investors in Shanghai who are banking on a rising market, making them a profit on paper before they have even had to make good on their deposits.

ROOM FOR SURPRISES

Cities are made by an extraordinary mixture of do-gooders and bloody-minded obsessives, of cynical political operators and speculators. They are shaped by the unintended consequences of the greedy and the self-interested, the dedicated and the visionaries. The cities that work best are the ones that keep their options open, the ones that allow the possibility of change. The ones that are stuck – overwhelmed by rigid state-owned social housing or by economic systems that offer the poor no way out of the slums – are cities that are in trouble. A successful city is one that makes room for surprises. A city that has been trapped by too much gentrification or too many shopping malls will have trouble generating the spark that is essential to making a city work.

The giant out- of-town sheds that are the predominant form of so many new cities now are not designed for flexible use or even for the long term. They are built with a maximum lifespan of 20 years in mind, and then trashed. Successful cities are the ones that allow people to be what they want. Unsuccessful ones try to force people to be what others want them to be. A city of freeways like Houston or Los Angeles either forces people to be car drivers or traps them in poverty. A successful city has a public transport system that is easy to use; an unsuccessful city tries to ban cars. A successful city has room for more than the obvious ideas about city life because, in the end, a city is about the unexpected. It's about a life shared with strangers and open to new ideas. An unsuccessful city has closed its mind to the future.

The nature of what we expect from the future is something that is very much

TOKYO, BEIJING, NEW YORK
PHOTOS: ANTONIA HENSCHEL

shaped by our personal trajectories. When I was an architecture student in the 1970s, there was a clear sense that the future meant Postmodernism: a rediscovery of the resonances of history and emotion. It was a moral certainty that attempted to offer an alternative to the moral certainty of Modernism. Both of them have fallen away, despite the best efforts of the Prince of Wales and others to present them as viable alternative futures. The fact, however, is clearly that the future is less predictable.

We are at a moment in which architecture is in the midst of a new period of uncertainty about its future direction. After a decade during which almost anything has been possible, during which architectural practice has been transformed in its scale and its technology, this is a time at which the world of architecture is looking for a more credible alternative. It will certainly be one that will in part be based on technology and its impact on how buildings are designed and how they are made. The way that architecture impacts on our consumption of energy and on the output of carbon is equally an issue. Indeed, these are issues that show every sign of becoming a latter-day form of Functionalism. Once form followed function, now it follows carbon footprints. The problem, of course, is that these relationships are far from being as clear as they sound. What really shapes the direction of form and its relationship to context is much less materialist in its inspiration. It is both a cultural idea of what architecture has to offer, and a technological one. We are, in many ways, at a moment very much like the one that Europe experienced a century ago, when Modernism and Rationalism wiped away the elaborations of Art Nouveau. It is a moment in which anything is possible, and in which we are ready to find new strategies.

Deyan Sudjic is Director of the Design Museum in London. His career has spanned journalism, teaching and writing. Deyan Sudjic was Director of the Glasgow UK City of Architecture program in 1999 and in 2002 he was Director of the Venice Architecture Biennale. He was editor of the magazine *Domus* from 2000 to 2004, and founding editor of the magazine *Blueprint*. Deyan Sudjic has published many books on design and architecture and he was made an Officer of the Order of the British Empire in 2000.

www.designmuseum.org

WE ARE AT A MOMENT IN WHICH ARCHITECTURE IS IN THE MIDST OF A NEW PERIOD OF UNCERTAINTY ABOUT ITS FUTURE DIRECTION. AFTER A DECADE DURING WHICH ALMOST ANYTHING HAS BEEN POSSIBLE, DURING WHICH ARCHITECTURAL PRACTICE HAS BEEN TRANSFORMED IN ITS SCALE AND ITS TECHNOLOGY, THIS IS A TIME AT WHICH THE WORLD OF ARCHITECTURE IS LOOKING FOR A MORE CREDIBLE ALTERNATIVE.

ON THE MOVE URBAN UTOPIAS OF THE MODERN AGE AND THE PRESENT DAY BY PHILIP URSPRUNG

Since antiquity, cities and mobility have been inseparably linked to one another. Cities always sprang up where transport routes intersected, where trade and markets were possible: near rivers, sea coasts, roads or bridges. They came into being in order to gain control over and ensure the security of these routes – their "life lines" (Lewis Mumford) – and they grew alongside them. Every type of city planning was therefore intended to enable and control mobility and, at the same time, to set the stage for it and lend it visibility. The rise of industrialization at the end of the 18th century served to reinforce this tendency. The acceleration of everyday life set in motion the development of materiality of the city itself. Emblematic for the utopia of the city in motion was the Première exposition des produits de l'industrie française, a city within the city that was erected on the Champs de Mars in Paris for three days in September 1798. This industrial exposition, the first of its kind, was a platform for the presentation of new, machine-made consumer goods. It marked a departure from the absolutist structures of the Ancien Régime, for example from the rigid system of guilds that prescribed which line of work a citizen was permitted to pursue. The exposition gave the starting signal for a still active tradition of industrial and world fairs, which function as testing grounds and experimental areas for architecture and urban planning. The exposition was a conglomeration of ephemeral market stalls that were dismantled after three days. Yet it was just this transitory quality that distinguished it structurally from the city's conventional form, and that heralded the modern city, which would serve as a stage for events. Since then, it has become nearly impossible to perceive the city as a self-contained conglomeration of static objects. The city is no longer understood as an object, but rather as a process, a vehicle of progress, a never-ending succession of interlocking events that are in a state of constant transformation.

The trademark of the Parisian industrial exposition was a tethered balloon. It simultaneously embodied industry's claim of triumph over the forces of nature and the goal of the young Republic to keep these brute forces in check. Visitors could float up into the sky in the tiny basket and admire the exposition from above. And from below, they could look up at the symbol of progress that offered a utopian indication of a new type of transport route – the airways. From then on, the conquest of the air would become an essential component of urban utopias and world expositions: from the observation towers flanking the Crystal Palace at the Great Exhibition of 1851 to the Ferris wheel at the 1893 World's Columbian Exposition in Chicago; from the moving sidewalks that transported visitors across the grounds of the 1900 Exposition Universelle in Paris to the chairlift at the Expo 2010 in Shanghai. All of these movable systems stand for the potential to extend mobility from a plane into the third dimension. They offer visitors and observers a hint of what might be. And at the same time, they position the exposition landscape in a perspective from which the utopia appears as something that has long since become reality.

THE CITY AS A MACHINE AND A FACTORY

While for the greater part of modern age the most popular metaphor for the city was that of an organism, in the course of Modernism its place was taken by that of the machine or the factory. New York, the epitome of a modern metropolis, is still known as "the city that never sleeps". Just before the outbreak of the First World War, Antonio Sant'Elia developed a project for a Città Nuova, a city that was entirely defined by overlapping layers of streets and in which the individual buildings loom like gigantic power plants. According to his manifesto *L'architettura futurista* (1914), the city should be "like an immense and tumultuous shipyard, agile, mobile and dynamic in every detail". Individual aspects of Sant'Elia's vision became reality in the elevated railways, factory halls, garages and docks that were built in New York, Moscow and Berlin in the 1920s. It was in the medium of film that it found its best expression. Films such as *Manhatta* (1921) by Paul Strand

THE CITY AS SCENERY OF A HORIZONTAL AND VERTICAL TRAFFIC FLOW: STILL PHOTOGRAPH FROM FRITZ LANG'S FILM "METROPOLIS", 1926.
PHOTO: AKG-IMAGES

AT THE CENTRE OF THE UTOPIAN CITY ARE TRAFFIC ROUTES: LE CORBUSIER, ARCHITECTURAL DRAWING: UNREALIZED URBAN PROJECT "PLAN VOISIN" (1922–25) FOR THE OLD CENTER OF PARIS ON THE NORTH BANK OF THE SEINE (RAZING OF THE AREA AND CONSTRUCTION OF 18 HIGH-RISES OF 60 STORIES)
FOTO: AKG-IMAGES / PAUL ALMASY

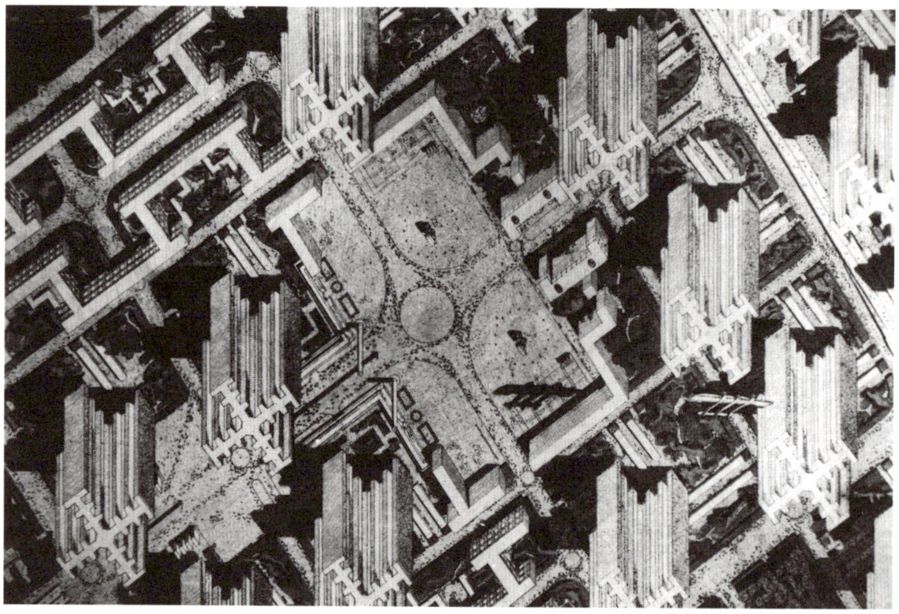

THE CITY AS AN IDYLL AND AGRICULTURAL PARADISE: FRANK LLOYD WRIGHT'S "PLAN OF BROADACRE CITY", 1934
CREDIT: ULLSTEIN BILD, GRANGER COLLECTION

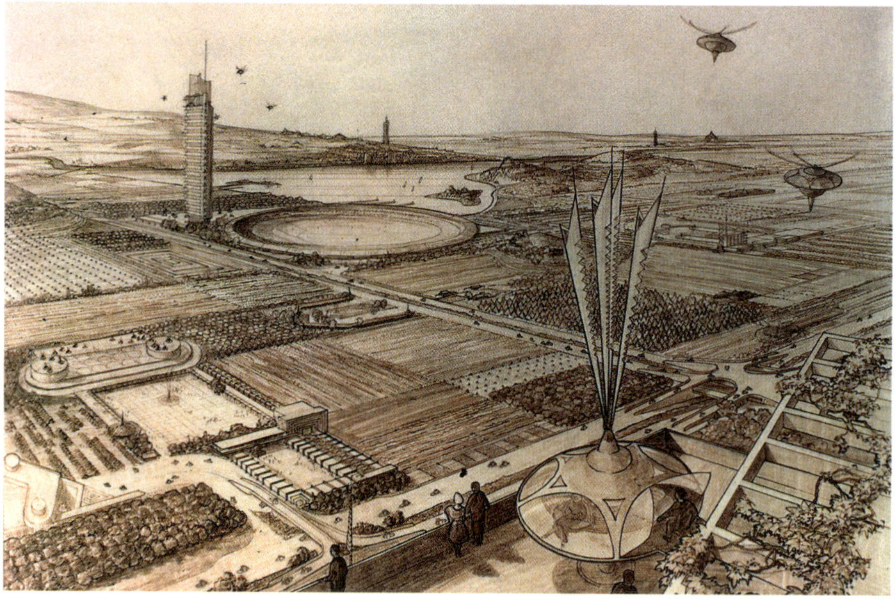

WHILE FOR THE GREATER PART OF MODERN AGE THE MOST POPULAR METAPHOR FOR THE CITY WAS THAT OF AN ORGANISM, IN THE COURSE OF MODERNISM ITS PLACE WAS TAKEN BY THAT OF THE MACHINE OR THE FACTORY.

and Charles Sheeler, or Walter Ruttman's *Symphony of a Great City* (1927) shaped the perception of the city as a moving image. In Fritz Lang's *Metropolis* (1927) and later in Ridley Scott's *Blade Runner* (1982) urban architecture ultimately became the backdrop for a never-ending flow of traffic that defined the urban realm as it moved through it both horizontally and vertically.

PARIS AS A METROPOLIS OF THE INDUSTRIAL AGE

Paris in particular experienced repeatedly throughout its history the fact that the movement of goods, people, or even troops is an engine for urban development. In the middle of the 19th century, the urban planner and Paris prefect George-Eugène Haussmann had entire city districts torn down in order to transform Paris into a metropolis of the industrial age. He constructed railway stations and infrastructure buildings, parks and broad boulevards that were intended, on the one hand, to facilitate control of the city and, on the other, to provide sufficient room for the increasing mobility of the prosperous bourgeoisie. As a radical continuation of Haussmann's projects, in 1922 Le Corbusier designed a plan for a Ville contemporaine for three million inhabitants. Once again, the Paris of the 19th century would have to make way for a contemporary city characterized by the demand for more rapid movement and yet denser traffic flow. Traffic arteries were again at the center of high-rise urban utopia. Le Corbusier provided for a separation of truck, automobile and pedestrian traffic, and allowed all of these roads to converge at a giant, central underground rail station with a platform for airplanes and air taxis. Frank Lloyd Wright, in turn, proposed an alternative to the city as a factory with his 1934 Broadacre plan, in which he designed the city as an agricultural paradise. The urban realm now appeared in the form of an all-encompassing rural idyll. Like Le Corbusier's city, it was accessible through a number of broad streets as well as by utopian aircraft that populated the airspace like a swarm of colorful insects. Wright naturalized urbanity and transformed it into a landscape of transportation.

BRASILIA OR THE VIEW FROM A MOVING AUTOMOBILE

Whereas during the economic crises these utopias existed only on paper, the dream of the modern ideal city became a reality in the prosperity of the 1950's. When the Brazilian city planner Lucio Costa was commissioned in 1957 with designing the new Brazilian capital from the ground up, he merged the ideas of Le Corbusier and Wright. The plan for Brasilia resembles that of an airplane and, interfused with green areas, the city was designed in such a way that it should primarily be navigated by car and be seen through the car window. In those days, the view from a moving automobile did, in fact, become a principle of urban planning. Kevin Lynch captured the essence of this tendency in his book *The Image of the City* (1960), in which he illustrated how industrial American cities like Jersey City and Los Angeles – so full of contradictions and defined entirely by automobile traffic – could be perceived as aesthetic phenomena and be articulated in a planning context.

THE CONFLICT OF VARYING SPEEDS

The formal coherency of Brasilia would prove to be too static to support the dynamism and complexity of urban development. As early as the 1960s, the first indications of what Rem Koolhaas ascertained in the middle of the 1990s began to emerge, namely, that there was a conflict "between the slowness of architecture and the volatility of the market". The discrepancy between the pace of machines and of humans preoccupied urban utopians in the 1960s and 1970s. Yona Friedman published the manifesto *L'architecture mobile* in 1958 and, in 1960, *La ville spatiale*. Friedman envisioned a megastructure, in other words a city that suited industrial reality. It was to be capable of flexibly adapting to the movements and requirements of its users. A static framework on high supports would be extended above existing cities, creating an infrastructure within which the individual parts could be continually changed. Cedric Price pursued similar goals in London in the 1960s. His project Fun Palace – a precursor to the Centre Georges Pompidou – was also a flexible megastructure that was intended to culturally reactivate the north of London, which was scarred by industrial decline and unemployment. Shortly thereafter, Ron Herron built upon Price's projects. In the magazine *Archigram*, he developed a plan for a Walking City, which foresaw mobile, highly engineered cities that would be able to move throughout the world and offer their services. The city should no longer be structured according to and around transport routes, but rather it should become such a route in and of itself.

THE CITY MOVES ITSELF

Several such Walking Cities could be interconnected as needed to form Walking Metropolises, and could separate again as soon as circumstances changed. The city of Skopje, today the capital of Macedonia, offers an impression of what these plans might have looked like in reality. Rebuilt following an earthquake in the early 1970s, the city is based on the concepts of the Japanese Metabolism

THE VIEW FROM A MOVING AUTOMOBILE AS THE BASIS FOR URBAN PLANNING: BRASILIA, DEVELOPED ACCORDING TO A PLAN BY LUCIO COSTA WITH THREE POWERS SQUARE AND BUILDINGS OF THE DISTRICTO FEDERAL BY OSKAR NIEMEYER, SHOWN ON A PHOTOGRAPH FROM 1965.
FOTO: AKG-IMAGES / PAUL ALMASY

A FLEXIBLE MEGASTRUCTURE APPROPRIATE TO INDUSTRIAL REALITY: THE RECEPTION ROOM OF THE APARTMENT OF YONA FRIEDMAN IN PARIS, 1974, WITH A CITY MODEL.
FOTO: AKG-IMAGES / PAUL ALMASY

movement, in other words on the idea that the urban realm is defined by a sort of metabolism of traffic routes. Some of the projects were never finished due to lack of funds. Yet even as a fragment, Kenzo Tange's train station offers evidence of the intention to generate the urban realm based on the logic of its traffic flow. The station was planned as a giant intersection for train, bus and automobile traffic. Today, the unfinished plateau recalls an abandoned aircraft carrier and marks the entrance to the city. All of these projects were developed at a time when classical heavy industry in Europe began to dissolve, when factories slowly began to disappear from the urban landscape and the information society's service industry took center stage.

DATA STREAMS DO NOT NEED AERODYNAMICS

In other words, they took shape as a new kind of mobility appeared on the horizon: the exchange of data via telephone and computer networks and the standardized exchange of goods by means of containers. Mobility could no longer be despicted adequately in the form of locomotives, automobiles or airplanes. And speed was now no longer necessarily linked to aerodynamics. Robert Smithson, whose work as an artistic consultant for a major airport project in Texas led to the invention of Land Art, was one of the first artists to critically reflect on this phenomenon. In his 1967 essay *Towards the Development of an Air Terminal Site*, he determined that for example satellites or, more specifically, the objects that move at the highest speed exhibit no trace of aerodynamic form, and he wrote: "Already certain passenger aircraft resemble pyramidal slabs, and flying obelisks. Perhaps aircraft will someday be named after crystals."

THE DISCONTINUITY OF THE CITY

The concept of the city has, of course, been altered in the course of de-industrialization, as well. Henri Lefebvre investigated the hypothesis of "the complete urbanization of society" in his book *The Urban Revolution* (1972). In his view, this society would emerge from industrialization as "the end of a process during which the old urban forms, the end result of a series of discontinuous transformations, burst apart". For him, the urban society was no longer determined by the parameters of industry – rhythm, repetition, multiplication – but rather by discontinuity, by "ruptures" and "difference". For him the form of this urban society posed a central question, which he left unanswered. The designs of Superstudio in the early 1970's might offer an impression of how Lefebvre imagined this "complete urbanization". To this day, like so many other projects from the 1960's and 1970's, they continue to challenge the theory and practice of urban planning.

Philip Ursprung, born in Baltimore, USA in 1963, has been professor for modern and contemporary art at the University of Zurich since 2005. He has taught at the Berlin University of the Arts, the ETH Zurich and the Graduate School of Architecture, Planning and Preservation at Columbia University in New York, and has also been a guest curator at the Museum für Gegenwartskunst in Basel and the Canadian Center for Architecture in Montreal. He is the editor of *Herzog & de Meuron: Naturgeschichte* (Montreal & Baden, 2002) and *Caruso St. John: Almost Everything* (Barcelona, 2008) as well as the author of *Grenzen der Kunst: Allan Kaprow und das Happening, Robert Smithson und die Land Art* (Munich, 2003) and *Die Kunst der Gegenwart* (Munich, 2010).

www.khist.uzh.ch

RIDING THE DATA WAVES HAVE THE DREAMS OF FREEDOM FADED? BY HEINRICH WEFING

We are probably only just beginning to understand how completely the Internet will change our lives. The American Internet theorist Nicholas Carr, author of the book *The Big Switch*, compared the effects that the Internet will have on all areas of our lives with the consequences of electrification just about one hundred years ago: "Electric light altered the rhythms of life, electric assembly lines redefined industry and work, [electrified media transformed the distribution of news and entertainment] and electric appliances brought the Industrial Revolution into the home. Cheap and plentiful electricity shaped the world we live in today. It's a world that didn't exist a mere hundred years ago, and yet the transformation that has played out over just a few generations has been so great, so complete, that it has become almost impossible for us to imagine what life was like before electricity began to flow through the sockets in our walls. Today, we're in the midst of another epochal transformation..."

Of course, no one really knows exactly what the world created by the Internet will look like. But there can be little doubt that the consequences of digitalization and networking will be felt in every corner of the world, in every branch of our lives. Already now, the way that we communicate, the way that we deal with information and how we perceive the world, is fundamentally different from what we were accustomed to ten or twenty years ago. Already now, the Internet has a massive impact on traditional media, countless industrial sectors and political culture. And if I'm not mistaken, the themes addressed by the *Audi Urban Future Award* – mobility and urban development – will soon be superimposed and permeated by the 21st century megatrend towards networking and digitalization.

NETWORKED DRIVING

At any rate, that was one of the central realizations of the first *Audi Urban Future Award* workshop held in London at the end of May. As constant as a base current, as persistent as a leitmotif, the concept that the car of the future will not be a metallic monad isolated from the world around it came up again and again in the participants' presentations. The automobile must inevitably become part of something bigger: the Internet. At times this idea was mentioned as if in passing, but occasionally it was very clearly enunciated.

The Internet has, without a doubt, long become the leading cultural medium of our time. It produces the metaphors of what is to come and dominates our imagination. Yet all shades of the utopian are conceivable. Alison Brooks of London, for example, asked the soberly pragmatic question as to whether the dashboard of an automobile could be transformed into a smart phone-like, versatile and mobile control unit, which drivers could program to meet their individual needs and could take with them upon leaving the vehicle. Brooks also played with the conceptual image that the car of the future could be plugged into the house of the future in much the same way that a USB stick is plugged into a computer – in order to exchange data, exchange energy, but also to coordinate the external appearance of house and automobile. And Brooks referred to already existing "intelligent" or web-based car-sharing systems that make it possible for users to find an appropriate vehicle in their proximity effortlessly via their smart phone.

DRIVING WITHOUT A DRIVER

If realized, another idea that was reiterated throughout the workshop in different variations would have a much more drastic effect on our conventional notion of driving a car: the concept of a "driverless car", as Bjarke Ingels of BIG in Copenhagen called it. He envisions a vehicle that not only does without noise or emissions, but also without a driver. Such an automobile, according to Ingels, could be navigated by an artificial intelligence, a computer that would prevent accidents and guarantee a more condensed traffic flow, which, at the same time, would be less prone to disturbance. In this way, as much as ten percent of the urban realm could be reclaimed for other uses.

AUDI URBAN FUTURE AWARD WORKSHOP
DESIGN MUSEUM, LONDON
PHOTO: SABINE REITMAIER, © AUDI

THE INTERNET HAS, WITHOUT A DOUBT, LONG BECOME THE LEADING CULTURAL MEDIUM OF OUR TIME. IT PRODUCES THE METAPHORS OF WHAT IS TO COME AND DOMINATES OUR IMAGINATION. YET ALL SHADES OF THE UTOPIAN ARE CONCEIVABLE.

A similar concept appeared in the "empathic vehicle" project presented by Enric Ruiz-Geli of the Barcelona firm Cloud 9. Thanks to highly advanced IT technology, his – also driverless – vehicle would react empathically to its user, the surrounding traffic and the city, to the natural environment and local climate. Zhang Ke of Standardarchitecture in Beijing also stated, albeit rather incidentally, that his individual vehicles, so-called "bubbles", would naturally be capable of navigating without a driver, at least within the massive Sixth Ring, with which Zhang Ke hopes to subdue the formidable traffic of Beijing.

The contribution of the Berlin-based architect Jürgen Mayer H. adopted the most radical treatment of the Internet paradigm. He sees the automobile of the future as being "fully digitized". Thanks to total networking, it will not only be capable of intelligently finding its way through the city without accident, but also will also act as the possibly most important interface between users and the network. "The automobile", according to his thesis, "will be transformed from a viewing machine for maneuvering in traffic into a sensorial experience machine." In his London presentation, the Berlin architect consistently implemented the image – both rhetorically and visually – of a traffic "current" that will be entirely transformed into a data current and like a tsunami will dramatically change the city.

AUDI URBAN FUTURE AWARD WORKSHOP
DESIGN MUSEUM, LONDON
PHOTO: SABINE REITMAIER, © AUDI

As Jürgen Mayer H. formulated it in his concept abstract, "Surveillance technologies will transform the city and its inhabitants into a flow of data, blurring the boundaries between body, car and architecture."

THE FUTURE OF FREEDOM

Obviously, such visions elicit questions – questions that are posed in the same or in a similar form anywhere the Internet is concerned. Roughly speaking, there are two issues that are closely related to one another: the question as to the future of privacy, and the question as to the future of freedom.

With regard to the first question: Who will provide the enormous computer capacity that will be required for the constant global fine-tuning of traffic flows? Who will finance them, and how? Automobile manufacturers? Internet giants like Google or Apple? Or the state? And furthermore: who will program the computers? Who will control them and, with them, the data tsunami? Who will control the controllers? Who will have access to the massive data quantities that would be collected every second of every day of every year? One doesn't need to be a pessimist to identify real and realistic risks to privacy here. If there are already justified concerns about the collection of communication data by the state today, how much more and more detailed information could be obtained through the exploitation of traffic data from millions of motorists?

Here's where the second question comes in, which focuses less on civil rights than on the "myth of the automobile" per se. In other words, what will become of the concept of freedom in the age of "driverless driving" – a freedom that is practically irrevocably linked to the automobile? What will become of the idea that the woman (or the man, respectively) behind the wheel has things under control, that freedom was something you could drive to in your own car? Alison Brooks called this legend back to mind impressively in her presentation. It was deeply ingrained in the pop culture of the 20th century, from Jack Kerouac's classic novel *On the Road* to films like *American Graffiti*, *Thelma and Louise* or *The Fast and the Furious*. The speedometer quivering, hair flying in the wind, the radio turned up full blast while outside the landscape speeds by – that is the iconic image of automobile freedom that has been reproduced thousands of times. Who would want to give it up?

The first answer is pedagogically strict: We can no longer afford this form of freedom. In an overpopulated, ecologically overburdened world whose resources are becoming ever more scarce, the individual use of freedom for the mere purpose of increased comfort is a nearly suicidal luxury that can no longer be justified. As nice as it was to glide along the Pacific coast on Highway 1 between Carmel and Big Sur, it is simply no longer possible. The dream is over.

HYBRID SOLUTIONS

A second possible answer, which one could perhaps call pragmatic and which is certainly much less restrictive, would be: We can still put the pedal to the metal and feel the wind in our hair, just not anytime or anyplace. There will be no clear-cut alternatives, but rather hybrid solutions: Far away from the city, out in the countryside where only few people live, there may every once in a while in the future still be the opportunity to drive fast, unregulated and on a whim – to be, to a certain extent, "free". In urban centers, in megacities and in their satellites, however, where space is limited and transport systems threaten to collapse, the freedom of the individual must be curtailed and controlled in the interest of the general public. During the London workshop, the thought periodically arose that only vehicles equipped for "driverless" navigation should be allowed access to urban centers, so that within certain zones traffic could be controlled by a computer cloud: cloud commuting thanks to cloud computing.

A third answer, perhaps the most radical and also the most difficult, could be that we must redefine the concept of freedom. Freedom would then no longer mean the possibility to get into your own car and drive from A to B at will, along whichever route, as fast or as slow as you want – and as traffic conditions allow. Freedom could be understood very differently: as the absence of stress, hustle and worry, as the freedom to converse, to read or talk on the phone, watch a film or take a nap while moving through the city. Freedom would then be the luxury of having your hands free while driving a car. And what's more, having your head free. At the same time, the concept of driving a car would gain new meaning. It would then stand for automated driving.

Heinrich Wefing, born in 1965, is editor of the political section of *Die ZEIT* in Hamburg. In the context of the *Audi Urban Future Award*, he moderated both the workshop in London and the award ceremony in Venice. Following his studies of law and art history, Wefing was an editor for the features section of the *Frankfurter Allgemeine Zeitung* from 1996 to 2007, first as a correspondent in Berlin and from 2002 to 2004 in San Francisco, and finally as head of the features office in Berlin. Heinrich Wefing has received numerous awards, including the Critics Awards of the Association of German Architects (BDA) and the Federal Chamber of German Architects (BAK). His next book, *Der Fall Demjanjuk. Oder Die Shoah vor Gericht* will be published this fall by C.H. Beck.

ALISON BROOKS ARCHITECTS

ALISON BROOKS ARCHITECTS
PHOTOS: SABINE REITMAIER, © AUDI

MUMBAI IN MOTION

CONVERGENCE AND EXCHANGE IN THE KALEIDOSCOPE CITY

"IN DEVELOPING COUNTRIES, THE 21ST CENTURY IS LIKELY TO BE THE SECOND AGE OF THE AUTOMOBILE."

MICHAEL LIND,
NEW AMERICAN FOUNDATION,
TIME MAGAZINE, MARCH 2010

In only forty years, the world population will grow by 39% to 9.3 billion. The number of people living in cities will increase from 50% to 75%. With the expanding wealth of developing nations, the number of cars could increase from 668 million today to three billion in 2050. Without a massive technology and lifestyle shift, the second age of mobility could come at a huge cost to both our ecosystems and the quality of life for the world's urban populations. This issue of the physical quantity of vehicles, their size and impact on urban land is one of the burning questions of our age.

The second issue is technology. What happened to the future of mobility? Our 20th-century space-age fantasies of personal mobility (i.e. flying cars) haven't materialized, but our deep-seated myths of car-based freedom, privacy, status and personal identity remain – cars are (very useful) Cultural Artifacts. But these myths are preserved at a huge cost: most four to six-seat vehicles are driven by a single occupant and although urban destinations are often shared, vehicle space, power and traffic management are not.

We are suffering from the results of early 20th-century car culture. We need a 21st-century mobility culture of convergence: integrating digital technologies, new compact car formats and community networks with wider public transport strategies to enable the world's mega-cities to grow in a sustainable way.

Smartphones are becoming universally accessible, even in developing economies. Soon millions of people currently cut off from economic mobility, education and knowledge will be able to access the world's information and social networks, and the world market. We can use this digital super-enlightenment to support new strategies for sustainable urban life – not only in the developed but also in the developing world's vast and over-crowded cities.

A greater choice of compact electric cars is needed to totally replace existing models that are polluting and over-crowding cities. Shifting the ratio of road infrastructure to green infrastructure will increase urban green and public living

ALISON BROOKS ARCHITECTS
PHOTOS: SABINE REITMAIER, © AUDI

space. Smartphones can act as portable, personalized car controls, freeing the car interior from the "dashboard" hardware so vehicles can act as a multi-functional, personalized living space. Web and smartphone-enabled peer-to-peer car or van-sharing can further reduce urban congestion. This is a microbusiness model for vehicle ownership that will generate new social ties and offer "universal" personal mobility. Car-sharing and renting open up huge possibilities for a new creative identity for mobility: how do I make my car more desirable for sharing than my neighbor's? The imagination runs wild!

ABA's proposition for the *Audi Urban Future Award* takes our ideas to the context of one of the developing world's biggest and densest megacities: Mumbai. Mumbai's culture, infrastructure, political and social institutions are deeply interdependent and local, but hold valuable lessons transferable to western cultures and "developed" urban systems. ABA proposes a strategic project of cultural exchange, a proposal for a sustainable urban extension to Mumbai, a density relief valve that builds on an existing "lifeline" of transport infrastructure.
By converging today's global technologies of enlightenment – personal digital devices with compact mobility, local community networks and cultural identities – we believe a mega-city in crisis can reveal the potential for a sustainable urban future: in motion.

Alison Brooks

www.alisonbrooksarchitects.com

Kaleidoscope City

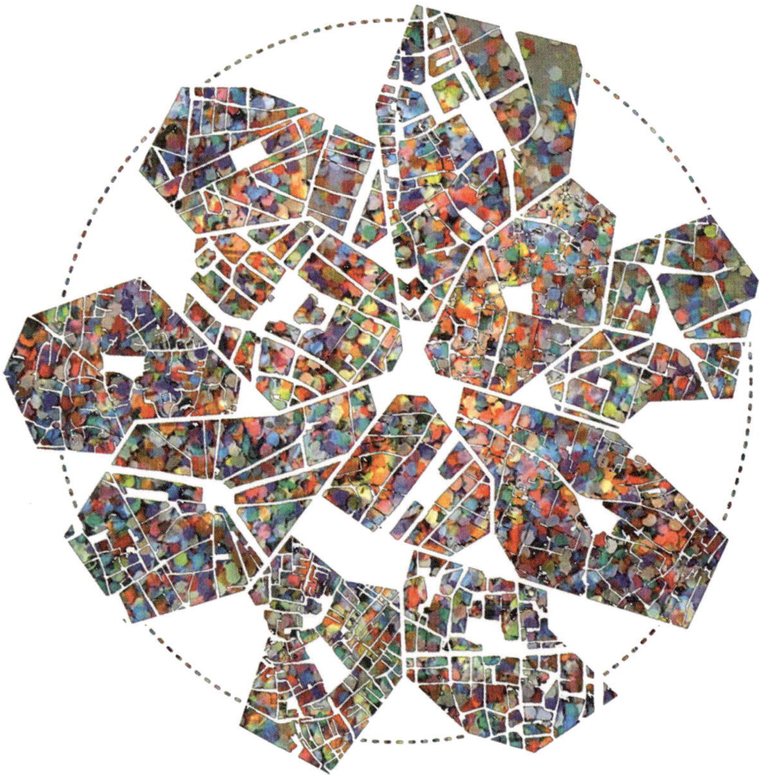

PRESENTATION ALISON BROOKS ARCHITECTS

ALISON BROOKS ARCHITECTS, © AUDI

Pimp my rickshaw?

Ganesh mobile

WHAT MAKES LIVING IN THE FUTURE SO APPEALING?

ALISON BROOKS INTERVIEWED BY VICKY RICHARDSON IN LONDON

Alison Brooks, Director of Alison Brooks Architects, explains why she decided to take up the challenge of considering a new future for mobility in cities. Brooks' approach is to consider the cultural identity of a place and find solutions that are highly particular and site-specific. Her work for the *Audi Urban Future Award* aims to find a new model for cities that is both physically dense and rich in social connections, but also aligned with ecology and nature. She does not rule out the car, but sees personal electronic devices offering a new future for mobility where automobiles will take up less space and become prosthetics for humans. Ultimately, Brooks questions the current defensive stance of architects and urges them to become public champions of urban and social transformation.

How would you characterize your work?
We're a practice in London that is involved in a wide range of projects, from small-scale domestic projects to large-scale urban masterplanning. What we try to focus on is the idea of drawing out identity and particularity from a cultural condition, which then informs our work. Every project is site-specific and through this approach we're able to push projects on several levels – structure, material and space – in a highly particular way.

Can you tell us about a couple of projects at the extreme of scale?
We're designing a house that is also an art gallery – an art gallery with people living in it. It's in the Forest of Dean on the border with Wales. I consider a project like this to be an opportunity to develop a thesis. It's a bit like writing a novel. You can explore ideas about space and landscape in a very particular way. On the other hand, we're doing a big regeneration project in South Acton in London. It's a masterplan for a large 1960s housing estate that's going to be demolished and rebuilt as a new piece of city. It's very much about knitting a new urban grain into a *tabula rasa* of 1960s planning. We're developing new kinds of super-hybrid buildings – urban food growing, housing, a library, a youth club – everything within one building. We're really interested in this idea of a strong mix of uses, a hybrid typology to urban housing.

Could you say that hybridization is what characterizes your work?
I don't like to limit the work to one characteristic, because architecture is never just one thing but is more pluralistic and inclusive. We do try to push hybrid programs, which lead to a new hybrid architecture. Traditionally, you get conflicting uses, but if you can bring them together it creates new opportunities for space.

Do you have a positive view of global cities, or do you think they are in need of transformation?
It's both: cities are in need of transformation. There's a need for densification and a global acknowledgement that we can't use land as extravagantly as we did in the past. But at the same time, I'm a complete urban dweller. I love cities, and I came to London twenty years ago from Canada because I love the intensity, diversity and the rich mix of cultures and languages that you get. I think really hard work needs to be done to reintegrate ecology and nature into cities, and to shift the priority from traffic and infrastructure to nature and people.

How have you approached the *Audi Urban Future Award*?
The first thing we did, which comes very naturally, was to think about how car culture and different types of mobility form part of the cultural myth of today. For example, we looked at the way that, in films, cars are often the main character. It's actually very rare that you have a film where cars, trains or planes don't feature. Then there are iconic films like *Bullet* or the Bond films – fantasy worlds, where cars are a crucial part of the image and the story and the characters. So we thought it important to realize how pervasive the brands of cars are. When you dig deeper, you realize that, actually, cars are a huge part of contemporary culture.

How do you think cities of the future will be defined in relation to mobility?

ALISON BROOKS AND VICKY RICHARDSON
PHOTOS: SABINE REITMAIER, © AUDI

CITIES ARE IN NEED OF TRANSFORMATION. THERE'S A NEED FOR DENSIFICATION AND A GLOBAL ACKNOWLEDGEMENT THAT WE CAN'T USE LAND AS EXTRAVAGANTLY AS WE DID IN THE PAST.

There is a general movement towards more compact and self-sufficient communities within the bigger urban realm: the idea of the polycentric city, where you can get most of what you need and live your life in a smaller neighbourhood. People can work closer to home, which fits into the idea of hybrid buildings that can be adapted for working and living. So you can get a lot of what you need in a walkable area, but you also have access to public transport, because it's good to get out, as well. Another important idea is downsizing: people could actually drive around in cars that fit their body, rather than having all sorts of additional space that isn't needed. We really think there's got to be a move towards smaller or extendable cars. You'd have the front end of your car and could plug in the back end at weekends and so, by reducing the size of the car, you could free up a huge amount of urban land. Those smaller cars could be integrated with smart and more effective public transport, for example car shuttles, where you drive your micro car on to a shuttle that zooms up to Manchester.

So our first idea is about downsizing mobility in order to free up land, which allows you to reinvent the city spatially. The second idea is that, once the control devices, networking and driving of a car become more or less hands free, then the car as a space has loads of potential

to be plugged into houses, to be an office or a workspace. Along with the principle that you have to have a more compact approach to development, cities will become more dense and you'll have to build upwards. We had the idea that if your car can become so small that it's more or less the size of a wheelchair, for example, then you could actually take your car with you in the elevator up to your home and plug it in. It becomes a flexible space that you can still use once you've brought it into your building.

What motivated you to go for this award and what do you think will come out of it?
We were really interested in the opportunity to think about city building and global urbanism as an extension of the work we've done in the practice, and that I've been pursuing since my thesis year in architecture school, which was about reinventing the centre of Buffalo in New York: dealing with these huge urban wastelands in the dead core of the city. Generally, I've always had a really deep interest in and concern for the bigger picture of how architects can make an impact at an urban scale, which has an impact on the quality of urban life for thousands – potentially millions – of people. Individual buildings are just one tiny bit of the story. This competition has given us an opportunity to broaden our research beyond a specific area in the UK or London, and to think globally. Working at that scale, but also looking at the quality of space inside an individual car or train or other form of mobility, allows for a really interesting dialogue because there is a lot of exchange – it is a symbiotic thing.

There's an elephant in the room with this award, which is the car. How has the fact that the award is sponsored by a car company influenced your approach?
We have tried to free our minds and just think about the impact of this development and research, without being attached to a brand or corporation. However, I think it's inevitable that we acknowledge the place that Audi has in contemporary culture and automobile manufacturing, and the potential of Audi as a patron of new technology, ideas and research.

Are there things that architects can learn from working alongside a car company in terms of the technology and approach to design?
There's definitely a potential for symbiosis. One of the obvious things is to do with power supply: as buildings become more self-sufficient energy suppliers, with photovoltaic panels or solar collectors, they will be able to supply power to electric cars. There's quite a direct potential there, we believe. Actually, there is a great deal of craftsmanship in automobile manufacturing. A whole economy of handmade things goes into cars, along with the GPS technology and electronics. The kind of human invention and skills that are required to put together cars draws on a huge social body, and that has a lot of value.

You've said before that you're interested in transformation. How could and should architects try to transform people's lifestyles?
It's our duty as architects always to think about how to improve the human condition, improve the quality of life and of our cities. The really big social issues have to be at the heart of what we do. Architects should come out and stake their claim and say what they believe in in terms of social projects. That was at the root of Modernism – there was a social project, and that is something that has been lost over the course of the 20th century.
At the turn of the 21st century, there was an obsession with buildings of extreme shapes that didn't have much to do with the human condition. Global warming and the environmental crisis have really been a wake-up call for the profession. Because we are so responsible for what gets built and how it gets built, architects can have a huge impact on the environment.

Do you think today there's an opportunity for architects to change things?
We architects don't have the voice that we should have in the public realm. You

DIFFERENT VIEWS OF THE MODEL
ALISON BROOKS ARCHITECTS, © AUDI

ALONG WITH THE PRINCIPLE THAT YOU HAVE TO HAVE A MORE COMPACT APPROACH TO DEVELOPMENT, CITIES WILL BECOME MORE DENSE AND YOU'LL HAVE TO BUILD UPWARDS.

virtually never read articles by architects in the paper unless some major new building appears. Or, an article covers a new building but doesn't even mention the name of the architect. Somehow, our role as social commentators has been diluted. There are very few architects who can be considered part of a political movement – maybe some of the Russian Constructivists. But this is also a very interesting time, with the new coalition government in the UK and the attempt to create bi-partisan progress in America in the face of huge resistance from the Republicans. The idea of collaboration in order to move forward socially and politically is great. It's a sign of the times in the new century that people can start to put aside their differences and work together.

Vicky Richardson was appointed Director of Architecture, Design and Fashion at the British Council in March 2010. She has previously had a successful career as a journalist, having been Editor of *Blueprint* from 2004–2010 and Deputy Editor of *RIBA Journal*. Vicky Richardson is a regular public speaker and chair of architecture and design events. She is a member of the London Mayor's Cultural Strategy Group, which advises on the British capital's culture policy, and a trustee of the educational charity The Campaign for Drawing. She has a degree in architecture from the University of Westminster and has also studied fine art at Chelsea School of Art and Central Saint Martins. Her writing is widely published and her books include *In Defence of the Dome* (Adam Smith Institute, 1999) and *New Vernacular Architecture* (Laurence King Publishing, 2002).

JUST WHAT IS IT THAT MAKES *TOMORROW'S* HOMES SO DIFFERENT, SO APPEALING?

ALISON BROOKS' IMAGES, CREATED ON COMPUTER, ARE A HOMAGE TO RICHARD HAMILTON'S FAMOUS COLLAGE OF 1956 ENTITLED "JUST WHAT IS IT THAT MAKES TODAY'S HOMES SO DIFFERENT, SO APPEALING?", WHICH HAMILTON MADE ON THE OCCASION OF THE EXHIBITION "THIS IS TOMORROW" THAT HE HELPED TO CONCEIVE AT THE WHITECHAPEL GALLERY IN LONDON.

ALISON BROOKS ARCHITECTS, © AUDI

2030
Mumbai
vacuum cleaning robot
POP
SHARE

BIG – BJARKE INGELS GROUP

BJARKE INGELS GROUP

LESS IS MORE

THE CITY OF THE POLLUTIONLESS, NOISELESS AND DRIVERLESS CAR

The futurist and inventor Ray Kurzweil describes the evolution in technology as an exponential curve following the *Law of Accelerating Returns*. Technological breakthroughs are happening constantly and occurring within exponentially shorter intervals! The speed of the microprocessor is doubling every 18 months, and we are approaching a true revolution in information technology, The Singularity. What if we applied the Kurzweil model to predict the evolution of the car?

The timeline for mobility starts with the invention of the wheel 11,500 years ago. Another 5,500 years pass before the next paradigm shift to the wheeled cart. A gradual series of technological advances eventually accelerated to the invention of the first "auto"-mobile in 1873. During the 20th century things speeded up: automatic transmission, highways, GPS navigation, and during the last decade we have seen the first breakthroughs in automated driving and safety systems. According to the graph, the car is rapidly approaching the next paradigm change in personal transport: the fully automatic driverless car. Cars that drive and navigate using robotic technology, organize in intelligent networks and make new use of the existing infrastructures in our cities.

If the rise of the automobile has been the single most influential event in the 20th century in terms of changing the geometry of cities, today it is causing some of the biggest challenges facing urban development globally: traffic congestion, air pollution, noise and CO_2 emissions. How will the rise of the electric pollutionless, noiseless and driverless car change the urban landscape? Infrastructure amounts to one third of the area in a typical European city like London. Are we using this area to its full potential? How much of the city could be liberated if cars could be packed closer and consume less space?

Could it be that the next revolution in urban space will be caused, not by flying cars, advances in speed or engine power, but by the full merger of information technology and personal transport? The driverless car, or true automatic mobility, could ignite the next revolution in urban space, changing not only the way we use our existing physical environment but how we plan for new urban life forms.

Bjarke Ingels

www.big.dk

BJARKE INGELS GROUP
© BIG – BJARKE INGELS GROUP

COORDINATING THE CHAOS OF MOVEMENT

BJARKE INGELS INTERVIEWED BY KENT MARTINUSSEN IN COPENHAGEN

According to the vision of Bjarke Ingels, founder of BIG, information technology will change the urban space of the future. The driverless car and collectively coordinated traffic will create an interactive, yet messy new form of urban life. The strict delineation of cars, pedestrians and bicycles will make room for more hybrid and flexible forms of urban mobility. That, in turn, will release a lot of spare capacity in the inner cities.

How would you characterize your work?
Our architectural ambition is pragmatic-utopian. Traditionally, architecture is dominated by two extremes: one that is very wild and expressive, but also expensive and unrealistic, and the other – which dominates most of the built world – that is practical and rational, but may also be boring, un-ambitious and uninspiring. We try to occupy the overlap between the two extremes, a place where we use all the different forces that flow through society – the cultural structures, the economic structures, infrastructure itself – as the driving force of the design. Architecture and cities are a continuous collective effort of trying to refurbish the surface of our planet so that it fits better with the way we want to live. What makes it interesting to be an architect is that we have the means to look at how life in the city happens and then try to create the framework around it. When life changes, so should architecture; when people inhabit the city in new ways, the urban space should adapt. In that sense, architecture is the art of translating human life into physical form.

What distinguishes your architecture from that of other architects?
We approach projects by analyzing how things have changed. Based on these changes – they could be economic or social changes – we try to come up with proposals on how this new way of human behavior informs a new architecture. Architecture is always being judged before it is realized. You have to present and communicate a project before it is built, get permissions, financing and so on. For an architect, a very crucial part of the process is showing how a project has grown out of society and these different demands and concerns. We try to establish which of society's demands and concerns make a project necessary or logical.

In your office there are a lot of models. Is volume important to you as an architect – the volume of working on a lot of projects at the same time?
I'm quite fascinated by Darwin's theory of evolution. It reflects the design process and the conditions of an architectural office, and also how cities and societies evolve. There are far too many ideas produced, far too many individuals are born, and only the more adept ones manage to pass their attributes on to the next generation. It's the same in the design process: we make a lot of proposals – some of them we drop, with some of them we carry on. We try to mate ideas, create offspring with a mix of qualities. Some of them become misfits, others become promising. We're very much based on the idea that architecture is like a midwife, that is has to assist society giving birth to itself. We normally start by analyzing the context: what the key issues could be in this context, what the problems could be, the potentials. Then, together with the team, I help establish what we should really look at. We have meetings about the research, and we try to turn it into ideas that we then start testing. It's very much like a process of natural selection.

So your job as an architect is more like an editor or curator than that of the classical architect who makes a sketch?
There is this cliché of the architect who is having dinner when, in some kind of divine intervention, he gets a brilliant idea. That is to elevate the architect to the status of a genius, but with no understanding or concern for human life and the artistic ideas that are forced onto people. The truth is that the architectural process consists of the much more careful and time-consuming effort to understand the conditions we operate in, and of trying to let them become the driving

force behind our designs. For us, architectural vocabulary is a means to an end. That end is to find new and better ways of helping human life unfold. Whichever shape, form, material or volume can do that the best, that is our preferred choice.

Most of your work is in the city. One could argue that cities represent both a challenge and a solution. What is your personal attitude toward the development of global cities?
Most of the European cities, Copenhagen included, look more or less the way they did a hundred years ago. But, of course, in the developing part of the world – China and Southeast Asia – you have this almost instant explosion of cities. The global financial boom created a sort of Bilbao-style urban development that is driven by spectacular centerpieces. Due to the financial collapse, some more long-term thinking has entered into the plans. Even in our more recent projects in China, we've experienced a departure from wanting the landmark to a desire for more sustainable urban development. We just submitted a new urban masterplan for the waterfront of Shenzhen, and our proposal was not so much to focus on creating an iconic statement, but more on envisaging a network of different forms of urban mobility.

Rather than rejecting these boomtowns, you're trying to find solutions, even for the kind of messy situations they create?
For an architect to resist the places where he is most needed would be silly. We can sit in Copenhagen and do beautiful infills on the pedestrian street in the medieval city, or we can get our hands dirty and try to inject quality into the chaos of cities of millions that is unfolding in China. With some rigorous thinking and careful planning, we can make sure that this new neighbourhood of Shenzhen is going to be more inhabitable and desirable from a human perspective than some of the Central Business Districts that you've seen pop up everywhere all over Asia in the last decades.

As an architect, can you have an impact on the political environment and an effect on politicians, who are the final arbiters of how the city is developed?
Being an architect is this incredible combination of having all the power and having absolutely none at the same time. You can do all the designs you want, but in the end it's always up to some other decision makers. A way of empowering the architect and urban planner is to stay alert to what the buzzwords in the political debate are. Right now, everyone is trying to be sustainable. You can see that everybody's trying to put a drizzle of green on whatever they are doing, in order to make it more acceptable. But you can also see some serious development, for example within the field of energy consumption. Urban mobility is very much an issue: how people actually move around in cities, and how the city accommodates the constant flow of human life.

If, in the past decades, cities have been defined by the automobile, it seems that now and in the future the structure of a city will determine which type of mobility it will accommodate. What do you think will happen in relation to mobility in cities?
We are involved in two parallel projects that deal with urban mobility. One is the study for Audi, and the other is a study for the city of Copenhagen called "The Ring City". The study for the *Audi Urban Future Award* is sponsored by a car manufacturer, and the Ring City project is triggered by the creation of a subway line on the periphery of Copenhagen. In both cases, you have to find a way of creating the best network of various forms of urban movement and of eliminating the resistance to changing from one form of urban mobility to another. Public transportation is not the problem and neither are bicycles or pedestrians – the problem is the cars. For Audi, we focused on ways of combining the desire for individual mobility with the need for some kind of collective coordination of all this free movement. There is quite significant potential for

BJARKE INGELS
© BIG – BJARKE INGELS GROUP

URBAN MOBILITY IS VERY MUCH AN ISSUE: HOW PEOPLE ACTUALLY MOVE AROUND IN CITIES, AND HOW THE CITY ACCOMMODATES THE CONSTANT FLOW OF HUMAN LIFE.

some kind of urban revolution in information technology and the advent of driverless cars. Audi already has self-parking cars. There are crash prevention systems that override the driver when they detect danger. Our prediction is that there will be driverless cars within 15 years. This means that once you enter the inner city, your manual override is disengaged and your car starts behaving in concert with the other cars. Individual transportation becomes collective transportation.

One of the challenges addressed by the *Audi Urban Future Award* competition is the development of the city with regard to traffic congestion. Your answer is not architecture as such, but rather conceptual thinking and new software?
The driving force behind what could be the biggest evolution in how our cities are inhabited and organized in the near future will probably be neither a new superconcrete or some even more impressive form of glass, nor a new architectural style. What will happen is that our cars will become more sophisticated. Information technology is where rapid development is still occurring – this idea of the driverless car, for example. Right now, our cities are governed by a sort of apartheid between the different forms of mobility, and cars are quite often described as some sort of evil phenomenon, forgetting that inside them are actually people who are trying to get on with their lives. If we could find ways of eliminating the barriers, that would be progress. We found a beautiful photo of the main street outside our office, from 50 years ago, where you have trams, automobiles, many bicycles and pedestrians, all moving around with hardly any restrictions.

Will that create better cities?
As soon as the cars start driving in concert, as soon as they are centrally coordinated, automotive traffic will become four times more compact than it is now. You won't have the traffic jams that you have now because you can retain a constant, organic flow. Right now,

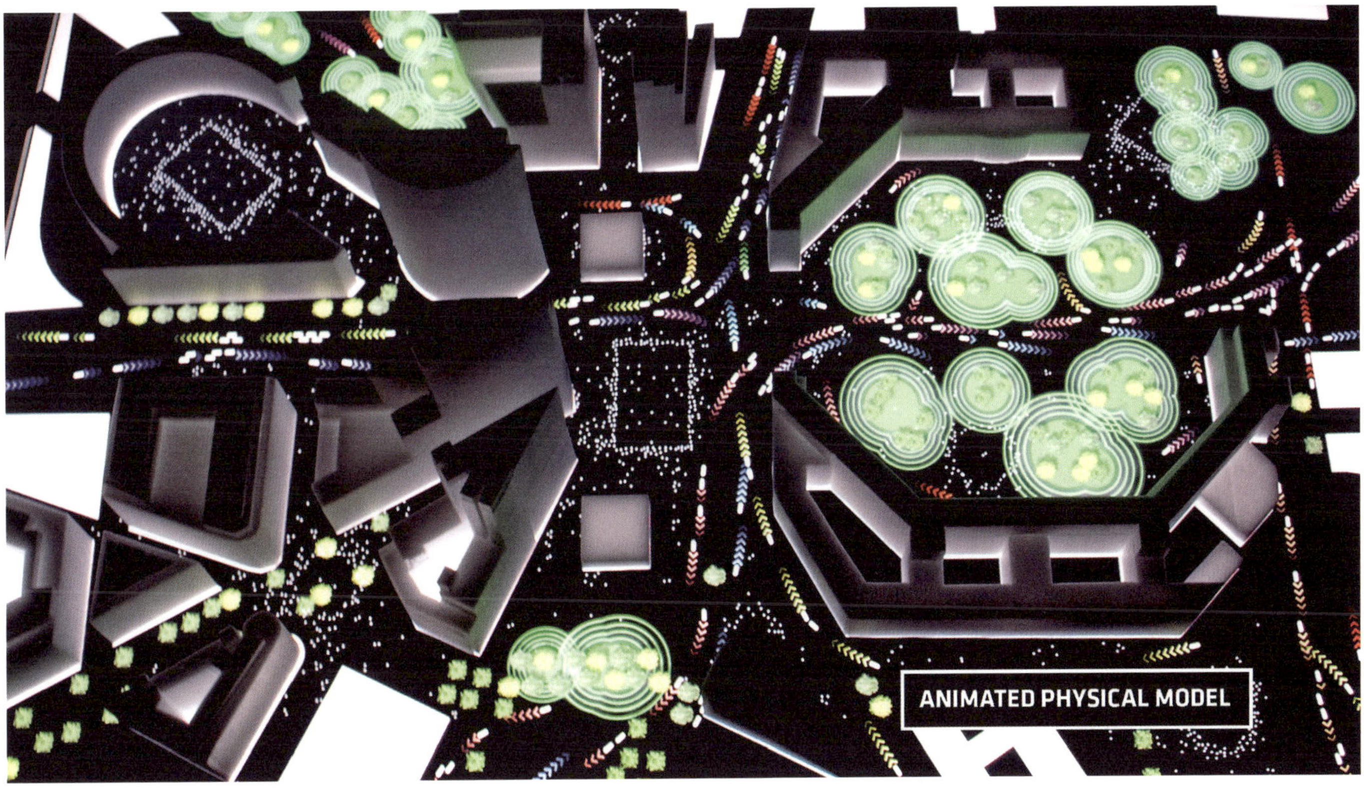

ARCHITECTURAL MODEL
BIG – BJARKE INGELS GROUP, © AUDI

city traffic is organized according to peak loads on certain roads and you can't really change the dynamic of the traffic easily just by changing the rules. What signifies a city as opposed to a highway is that you have smaller car lanes, but a much more finely attuned network of streets. By having a central coordination, you can actually direct how streets are used at different times and you don't have to use signage to do it, because the cars will know automatically. This sort of coordination is going to release a lot of spare capacity in the inner cities. It means that the same street can change from being full with pedestrians to cars or mixed use at different times. Here in Copenhagen, along with the main network of pedestrian streets, there is one street that has mixed traffic. Pedestrians have priority, but cars are allowed to go there, and so are bikes. It all happens with respect for pedestrian life. So you have this street with no strict delineation of who goes where, with café tables occupying part of it, and you also have cars that carefully weave between all the other forms of public life.

So that's the future? And how does the fact that Audi is the sponsor of the *Urban Future Award* affect your vision of the future?

Yes, that could be the future. We found it kind of funny that Audi had commissioned this urban study. But, you may know the famous "Plan Voisin" by Le Corbusier, this vision of a future city of parks and highways and high rises? It was commissioned by the French car and airplane manufacturer Frères Voisin. So, one of the most iconic studies of urban Modernism was done on behalf

BUT THEN WE STARTED CONSIDERING A LESS MINIMALIST AND CLEANED-UP VISION OF THE FUTURE CITY. THE DRIVERLESS CAR AND TRAFFIC THAT'S COLLECTIVELY COORDINATED BY INFORMATION TECHNOLOGY COULD ACTUALLY HELP CREATE A MORE INTERACTIVE AND MESSY NEW FORM OF URBAN LIFE.

of a car manufacturer. I didn't know that until we started the design process for the *Audi Urban Future Award*. Audi being a German company, our first thoughts were inspired by the cultural heritage of Mies van der Rohe: that "less is more". And the driverless car fits that conceptually. But then we started considering a less minimalist and cleaned-up vision of the future city. The driverless car and traffic that's collectively coordinated by information technology could actually help create a more interactive and messy new form of urban life. So our vision is more along the lines of "mess is more" rather than "less is more". The more sophisticated the coordinating technology, the more free and more varied the forms of social intercourse will be that we're going to see taking place in the cities of the future.

Kent Martinussen, born in Copenhagen in 1960, trained as an architect at schools in Paris and Milan and at the Royal Danish Academy of Fine Arts in Copenhagen. He has run his own architectural firm and taught and researched at universities and schools of architecture in Denmark and abroad, and has given talks at the International Architecture Exhibition in Venice and at architectural triennials in Japan and the Middle East. Kent Martinussen was a member of the international jury of the 9th International Architecture Exhibition in Venice and chairman of the award committee of the Nykredit Architecture Prize. Since 2001, he has been Managing Director of the Danish Architecture Centre (DAC). He and his fellows from the DAC received the Golden Lion at the International Architecture Exhibition in Venice for Best National Pavilion in 2006.

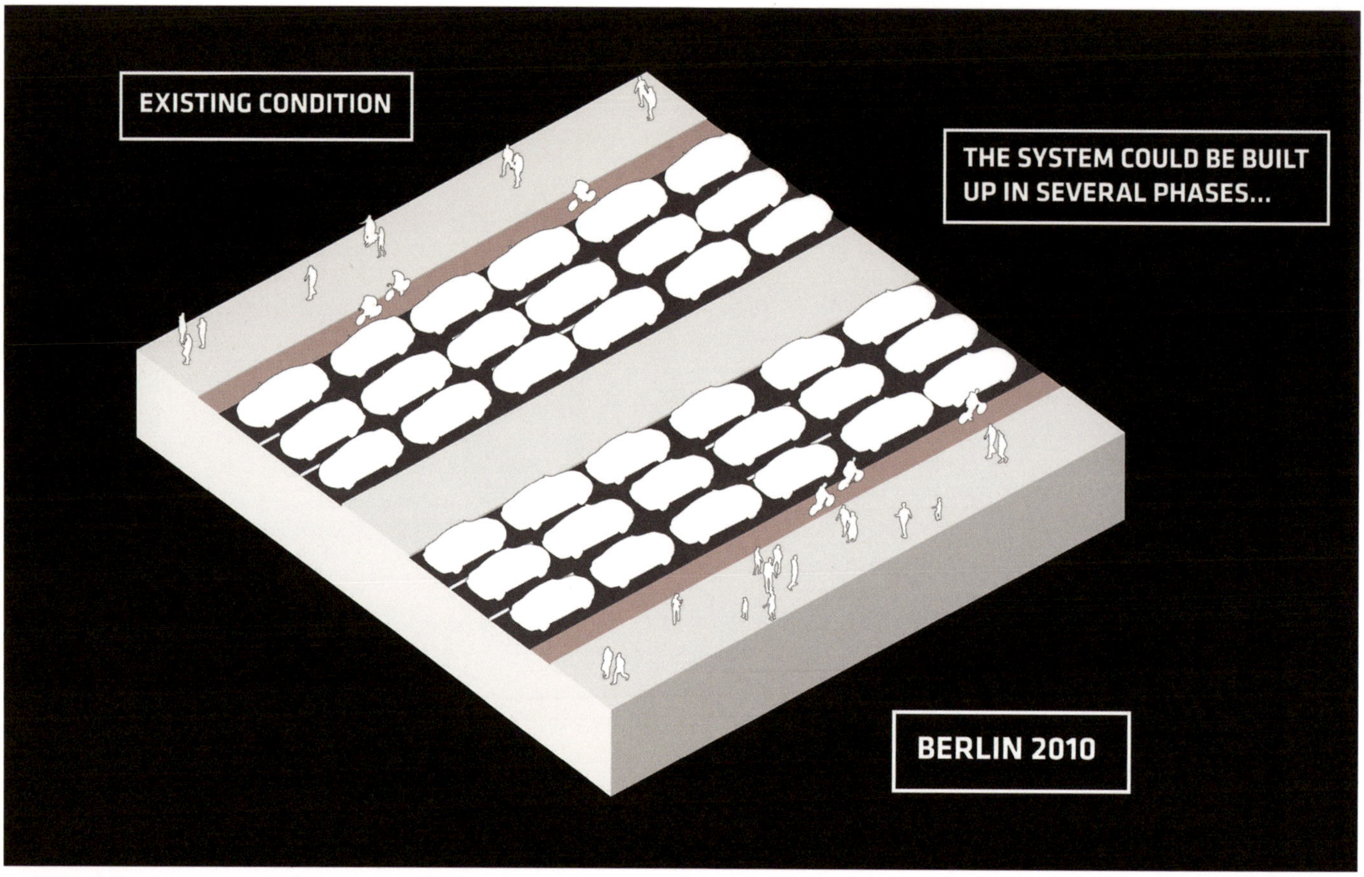

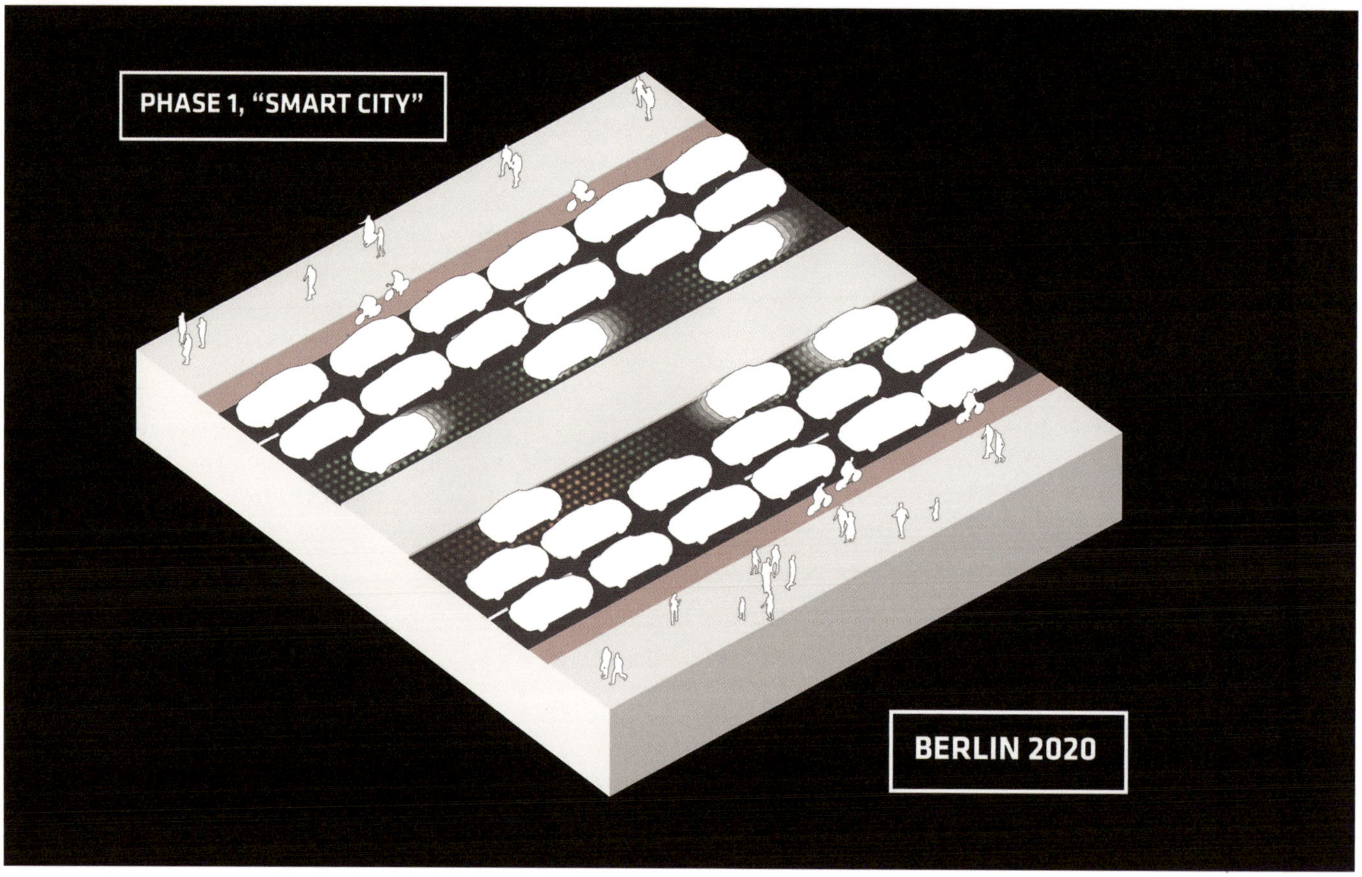

PRESENTATION BJARKE INGELS
BIG – BJARKE INGELS GROUP, © AUDI

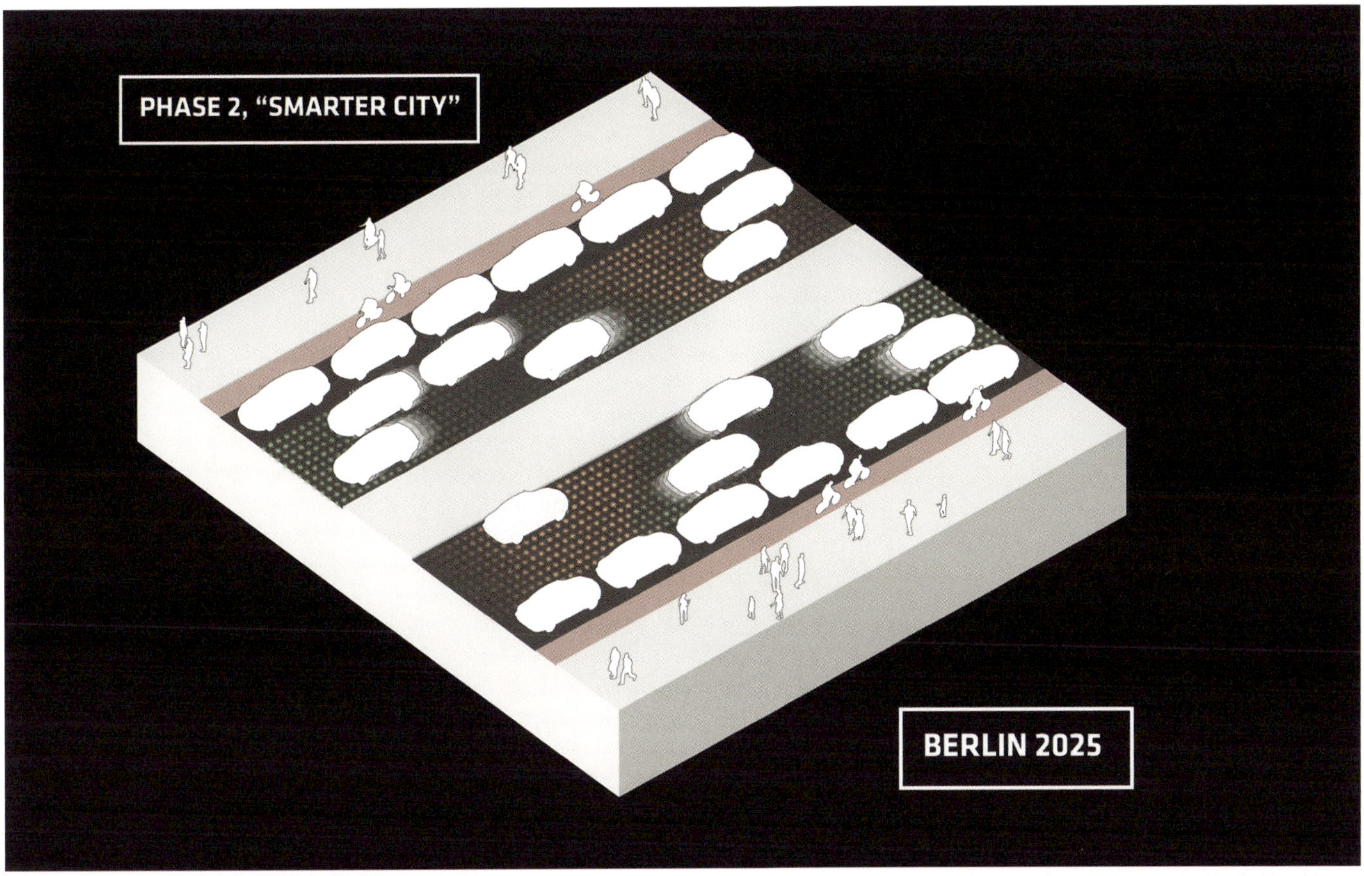
PHASE 2, "SMARTER CITY"
BERLIN 2025

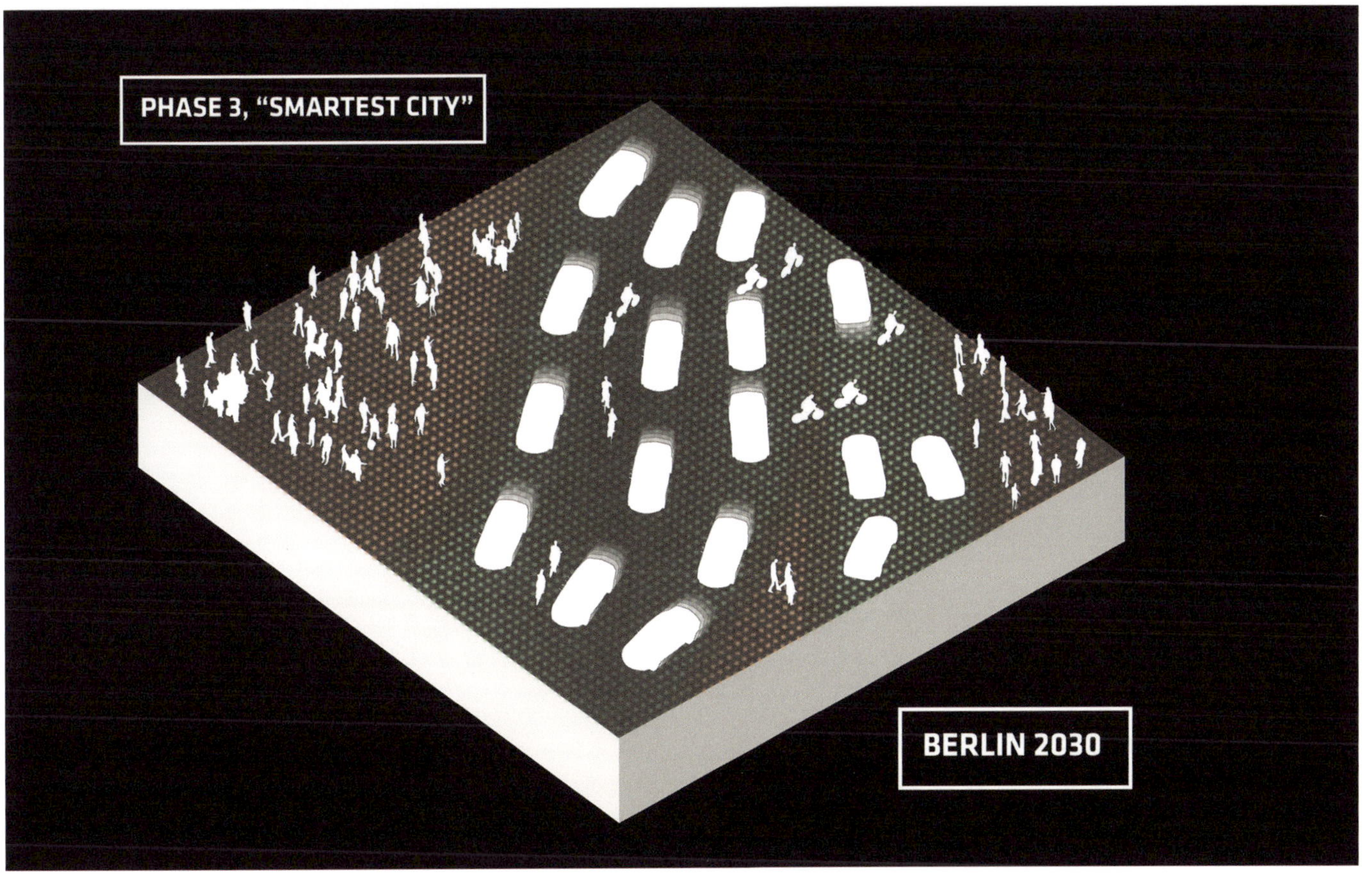
PHASE 3, "SMARTEST CITY"
BERLIN 2030

HOW WILL THE RISE OF THE ELECTRIC POLLUTION-LESS, NOISELESS AND DRIVERLESS CAR CHANGE THE URBAN LANDSCAPE?

ARCHITECTURAL MODEL
BIG – BJARKE INGELS GROUP, © AUDI

CLOUD 9

CLOUD 9
PHOTOS: SABINE REITMAIER, © AUDI

BARCELONA'S EMPATHIC CAR

1. City and cars in 2030.

2. We have invited children from the age of 8–10 to design with us as a collaborative team.

3. These kids will be 28–30 years old in 2030; therefore they will be decision makers.

4. We strongly believe that intense experience creates knowledge.
Note: I am an architect, maybe because my parents built a house when I was 8 years old.

5. Progress is a long-term process.

6. It will start now with these children – and in order to be successful we must involve them from the beginning: from being thinkers to being conscious users later.

7. Jeremy Rifkin's *Sustainable Design Team*, of which I am part, and the Third Industrial Revolution CEO's Round Table (e.g. IBM, HP, Acciona, Bouygues, Schneider, Philips), all agree that there is one model, one scenario, one technological platform which is where the city is going in the years from 2015 to 2050:

8. Pillar ONE: clean renewable energies
+
Pillar TWO: buildings as power plants
+
Pillar THREE: hydrogen technology and fuel cells
+
Pillar FOUR: smart grid

9. Cities produce 80% of global CO_2 emissions.

10. Buildings produce 40% of global CO_2 emissions.

11. In Barcelona we have created the Media ICT building.

12. It performs a reduction of 37% in CO_2 emissions.

13. Europe wants to achieve a 20% reduction by the year 2020.

14. The Media ICT is a "bubble" building where a membrane protects the building from the sun's radiation and creates a sun-filtering factor of 0.20.

15. We must go from geosphere politics to biosphere politics, in order to create an empathic civilization where cities, cars and people create an empathic environment; together they add, they balance, they merge and finally create a new nature that emerges.

16. Nature needs protection, needs technology, needs help.

17. People need protection, need technology, need help.

18. Nature needs a bubble, people need a bubble.

19. Could a bubble be a car?

20. We do not know what is the basic car to start with: Is it electric? Is it a hybrid car?

21. But we know it has to be light, and we know it has to be flexible to absorb the energy from a possible crash. So it is about fiber glass, carbon fiber...We are looking towards energy self-sufficiency. We would like to imagine a soft skin with photovoltaic dots which contribute to the energy production. We would like to conceive architecture and cars with a defined local climatology. We would like to recycle the rainwater to produce drinkable water. We would like a post-oil era using electricity and hydrogen as the main power sources. We would like a flexible skin made of ETFE (ethylene-tetrafluoroethylene) to allow "morphing" possibilities of the interior space.

22. Somehow it is not a car + airbag + people but an airbag-car + people.

23. The final aim is to join science led by Jeremy Rifkin and fiction led by Pep Bou towards research on beauty: Barcelona's Empathic Car.

Enric Ruiz-Geli

www.ruiz-geli.com
www.themakingofcloud9projects.com

The Institut Ramon Llull is dedicated to the promotion of the Catalan language and the culture of the areas in which Catalan is spoken. Thank you for your support:

www.llull.cat

CLOUD 9
PHOTOS: SABINE REITMAIER, © AUDI

THE WORLD AS A BUBBLE: VISIONS BY CLOUD 9
CLOUD 9, © AUDI

LIVING THE ENERGY TURNAROUND

ENRIC RUIZ-GELI INTERVIEWED BY SANDRA HOFMEISTER IN BARCELONA

Enric Ruiz-Geli of Cloud 9 has a clear concept of the city of the future: it will be powered by clean energy, even produce energy itself, and it will be organized as a dynamic platform upon which architecture and automobiles, people and buildings will be networked together and will communicate with one another. The role of the architect should be that of a humanist, developing new technologies in collaboration with various partners and suggesting how they can be implemented in an urban context.

Which aspects do you consider essential for today's cities, in either a positive or a negative way?
Cities generate 80% of the CO_2 emissions to the atmosphere. Therefore, cities are crucial. In our fight against global warming, cities are the answer and the problem. Cities have big potential and lots of possibilities in terms of human resources. But they are going to collapse under the pressure of mobility. Energy is the driving force for both global warming and mobility. Hence, we must change mobility, maybe by just changing the energy it uses, and we must change the basic energy structure of cities. The question that immediately arises in that context is: Who is going to be able to operate quickly and efficiently on this large scale in the next years?

Your point of view is related to the whole structure of society. Where do you see hints of the future in today's discussions on urban development?
We are in an economic, financial, social and environmental crisis – all these feed into each other. The old model of the city will collapse – this fact is important in order to create new models of urban spaces. I am sure that the future city will not look the same as today, because it will be created on the basis of a new consciousness. You can already observe this consciousness arising more and more nowadays. It is the mindset of a society that wants to know exactly where the energy comes from. People want to empathize with a new city. Thus, I am convinced that the concept for our cities will be that of a dynamic and vital platform that collects and creates new qualities from urban density.

What does this mean in terms of consequences for the future transformation of the urban space?
Our concept of urban space needs to integrate the idea of a smart city. In terms of communication, we have had a revolution with smart phones; in terms of building processes, we have robotics and other fast fabrication techniques. But we haven't integrated smart technology and intelligence for the urban space yet. As a consequence, our cars do not communicate with the street, the street does not communicate with our homes and our homes do not communicate with our cars. There is no network between the single urban elements at all. I guess the biggest step towards the future transformation of the city will be for urban spaces to activate their sources of communication and networking. That means that people talk to each other, objects talk to each other and buildings talk to each other.

Mobility was a driving force in defining the city's structure in the 20th century. Maybe this correlation will be reversed, and the structures of cities will define the kinds of mobility in use. Has this thought influenced the scenario you are developing for the *Audi Urban Future Award*?
In our strategy, mobility is neither the input nor is the city the output, or vice versa. There is no A and B, in fact, but rather a continuous flow of information and a relationship between the city and mobility in terms of A B A B A B A…
When electric cars are placed in the city, this will of course have consequences on the whole urban system. Vice versa, a dense city affects mobility, which speaks for electric cars. In reference to buildings, one cannot think of architecture without engineering; engineering and architecture go together.

Do you rely on any particular theoretical background for your future vision?

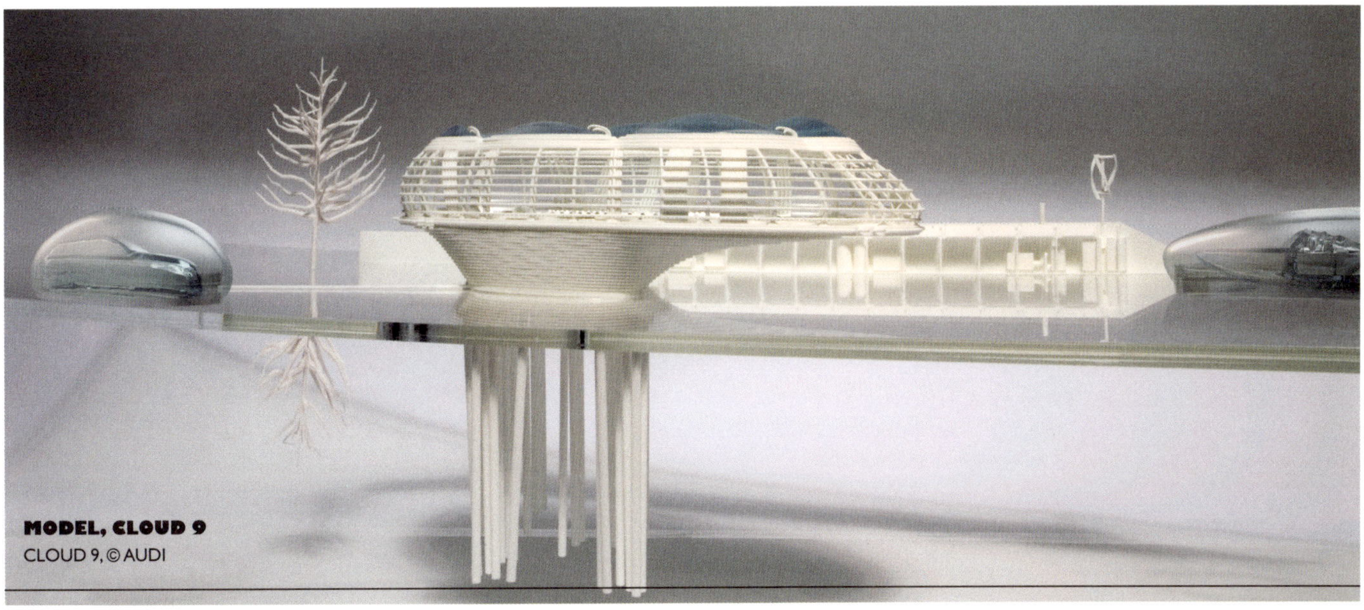

MODEL, CLOUD 9
CLOUD 9, © AUDI

We need more storytelling in this context, and I think Jeremy Rifkin's *Third Industrial Revolution* helps a lot. Rifkin proposes four pillars as objectives in his theory, and the city is deeply implicated by those arguments. The first pillar is clean energy: We are the last oil people and I do not want our kids to be part of that. The second pillar is that buildings are the solution to global warming. We can – yes we can! – construct buildings that only consume the energy they produce, that are off-grid and self-sufficient in terms of energy. The third pillar: We need a medium with which to realize our ideas about new energy systems. The car industry, of course, has an important role in this context. And the fourth pillar is smart cities, smart cars, smart mobility and smart living. All this together will create a new humanism based on the concept of empathy. The discussion is not whether the city will affect mobility, or vice versa. They are both tools and systems. What we put into the systems is what is important to us: our objectives.

During the design process for your contribution, you proposed an empathic car for a post-oil future society. What is the conceptual range of that?

At the beginning of the design process for our contribution to the *Audi Urban Future Award*, we invited kids to participate in developing ideas for the future. In 20 years, those kids will be mayors. Therefore, a vision of future mobility has to contain their ideas. We were very astonished at the clear prospects those eight-year-old kids had: They suggested air as the driving force of the car.
We also had engineers participating in the workshop, sociologists, biologists and architects, but none of them could offer serious opposition to the children's dream of a car driven by air. And in the end, the world has biodiesel, gas, oil and electricity-driven car engines. Why shouldn't there be air in the future as well?

Is that approach – starting with a dream – the basis of what you call "empathy"?

Yes, indeed. Our focus is on empathy that is created by human resources. Therefore, humans are our starting point – individuals or collective groups, couples or families. We will see how the design

ELEMENTS OF A FUTURE CITY

CLOUD 9, © AUDI

ENERGY

PILLAR ONE. CLEAN ENERGY

01 Wind turbine, GREENURBANENERGY
4.2m x 2.75m, height: 5.5m
Rated Power: 4kW
Rated Wind Speed: 12m/s
Noise Level at 3 Meter Distance: 27– 37dB
Production: 1,5 kW

02 Photovoltaic Lights, Cloud 9, Iguzzini
Technology: poli-cristalline silicius
LED: TOP LED RGB OSRAM 4X 0.4W
Total Wattage: 5W
Battery technology:lithium-ion
CPU w/ custom made operating System
Weight: 800 gramm, Dimensions: 34,5cm

03 District Heating and Cooling, Grupo JG
Heating / Cooling energy demands can be reduced by 35% when a network to factories is established that produce heat as a side product.

04 Geotermia, Tecnalia Energia
Geothermal heat is absorbed through heat pump which satisfies 0.07% of global primary energy consumption

PILLAR TWO. BUILDINGS AS POWER PLANTS

05 ETFE skin, Vector Foiltech
Reduction of solar gain: through the use of the fog system the coefficient of thermal conductivity is lowered by 8% to 29%.
CO2 emmisions are reduced by 60%.

06 Photovoltaic Cells, Tecnalia Energia
Technology: poli-cristalline silicius
Costs: 2 Euros per Watt
Lifespan: about 30 years
Potential of total installation: 12.02 kWp

07 Green Roof, Bures Innova
A green roof for a room of 120 m³ can decrease indoor temperatures by 5,1°C and provide a cooling potential of 3.02 kWh per day.

08 Hydroponic Mesh, Cloud 9, Bures Innova
CO² consumption: 15kg of CO² / m² / year
Air Quality: Pollutants are caught by plants and then transmitted to substrate by the plants metabolism.

PILLAR THREE. HYDROGEN STORAGE

09 Hydrogen Storage, Hydrogenics
Intermittent Energy is converted to Hydrogen. Hydrogen as an energy carrier can reduce the release of pollutants or greenhouse gases at the point of end users.

PILLAR FOUR. SMART GRID

(((• Monitoring Nature Sensors, Andreu Catala
Data like movement, climate conditions, sun orientation and humidity are collected to increase energy performance of buildings.

ip IP addresses, Siemens, Schneider
An electronic device added to energy producing and consuming units can obtain information on how to decrease peak energy usages and when to sell energy at times demands/prices are high.

nfo Social Robotics, Andreu Catala, UPC
In addition to IP devices and monitoring of nature social robots may inform users about status and performance of buildings.

clean Cleaning Robotics, Fatronik
Robots are introduced to perform regular inspection of used technologies and to clean for example the solar panels

MOBILITY

A WALK
Human walking. Individual mobility

B CARS
Automotive mobility powered by electric or hybrid powertrains. Includes all types of vehicles such as:

- B1 electric and hybrid cars
- B2 SUV
- B3 4x4
- B4 family cars

C MOTORBIKES
Mobility based on Motorbikes or individual motor 2 wheel drive vehicles(energy & internal combustion energy).

D INDIVIDUAL-UNITS(ELECTRIC POWERED)
Auxiliary electric individual mobility units, driven manually by a single person. Electric powered drivetrain.

E BIKES
Two wheel individual mobility system, using only pedaling effort from the user:

- E1 Bicing
- E2 electric bike
- E3 private bikes

F BUSES
Wheel road public transport units powered by both Hidrogen and fuel sources of energy. For small size units, 100% electric vehicles should be available.

- F1 public bus
- F2 school bus

G TRAIN
Surface transport rail system powered by electric energy both battery storage and wire connected.

H BOAT
Automotive mobility powered by electric

- H1 hybrid drive Yatches
- H2 greenpeace boat
- H3 windfources
- H4 kite-Surf

I AIR TRANSPORT

- I1 Solar powered Airplanes
- I2 Parachutes
- I3 Hot Air Balloons
- I4 Hang gliding
- I5 Gliding (unpowered airplanes)

J TRACTORS

	Rambla (urban area)	Media TIC	Villanurbs	Wave	Aviary	Figueres
A Walking\ trecking	●	•		•		•
B Cars	●	•	•		•	•
C Motorbikes	●	•		•	•	
D Individual-units	●	•				
E Bikes	●	•				
F Buses		•			•	•
G Train		•			•	
H Boat			•	•		
I Air transport						•
J Tractor						•

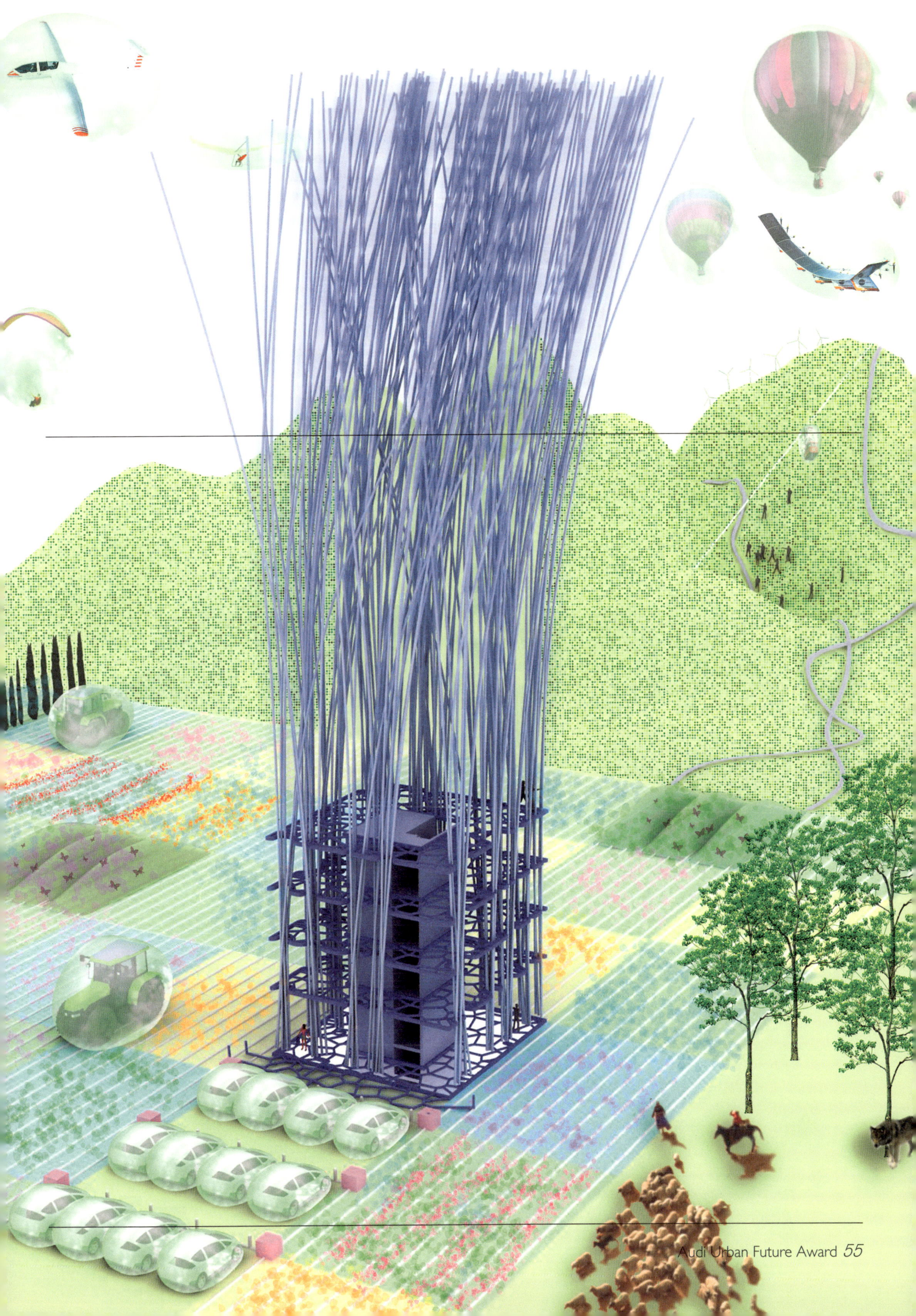

I AM SURE THAT THE FUTURE CITY WILL NOT LOOK THE SAME AS TODAY, BECAUSE IT WILL BE CREATED ON THE BASIS OF A NEW CONSCIOUSNESS. YOU CAN ALREADY OBSERVE THIS CONSCIOUSNESS ARISING MORE AND MORE NOWADAYS. IT IS THE MINDSET OF A SOCIETY THAT WANTS TO KNOW EXACTLY WHERE THE ENERGY COMES FROM. PEOPLE WANT TO EMPATHIZE WITH A NEW CITY.

ENRIC RUIZ-GELI AND
SANDRA HOFMEISTER
PHOTO: SABINE REITMAIER, © AUDI

evolves. I'm very sure we will have a strong relationship between the house and the car. However, in a next step, we consulted an artist who designs bubbles. He is a professional bubble maker and knows all about the physics, the membranes and the surface of bubbles.
In order to experience being inside a new car, we got inside a huge bubble with him. And then we suddenly realized that the car and the bubbles do the same job: They protect us from the outside, against rain and weather conditions, and they can protect the environment as well. That's a good objective, I think. And with that perspective, our empathic bubble car was born. Today, we are linked to a research center to explore possibilities for the engineering structure of such a car, we are cooperating with an ETFE manufacturer to work on this, and we are looking at photovoltaic particles that can be printed on the ETFE foil. We have had very good experiences with ETFE, even in terms of sustainability. Why shouldn't we consider a car made of polyethylene-co-tetrafluoroethylene plastics as well? In this concept, the skin becomes an airbag – the car itself becomes an airbag. What is important for the car is the experience of being in a car. And of course, with a translucent ETFE skin, you can have a much more empathic experience than in today's automobiles. The empathic car is much more closely related to nature. It will be balanced within a new system of energy, it can be self-sufficient and, in our vision, it is directly related to the house. Last but not least, it is a local car in terms of its energy supply – that's an important aspect. We call it the "Barcelona local car".

Audi is sponsor of the *Urban Future Award* – has the fact that an automotive company is the sponsor of the award influenced your ideas?
We believe that sponsorship is not a flat and simple relationship. We consider Audi to be a partner in a research and technology network. As architects, we have access to the technical team and the research capacities of Audi. We also went to Ingolstadt to get to know the company better. There is a lot of feedback from Audi, and we see the company as a partner in developing technology with additional values. They make cars to please people. We make buildings to please people, so we are on the same side in a win-win relationship. Furthermore, our relationship to Audi in this project can have an influence on an important question: Maybe an automotive company can take the initiative for a first step in the upcoming energy revolution.

What about the organization and structure of the urban space – in which direction will they change and what is the role of the "Barcelona local car" in this?
We are moving forward from geopolitics to biosphere politics where the city and mobility are concerned; therefore buildings must be self-sufficient in terms of energy. They can collect wind and solar energy. In addition, they will have tools like green roofs and better insulation. Our aim is to reduce the energy consumption of buildings by 40%. The other 60% will be achieved by clean energy, such as local geothermal sources. The car plays a significant role in this: It can function as a storage unit for energy for the house and as a kind of hydrogen battery for the whole system, which would collapse without a car. As a consequence, the car is not only important for mobility, it is the battery that is required by the system. High technology, energy and so on – all this can be integrated into the car and linked to the architecture. Thus, we don't want to chase the cars out of the city, we want them to play a prominent role in a new energy system. Consequently, cities will be greener. We will have more nature, less need for urban sprawl. Nature will be integrated into the city; the streets will have orange trees, agriculture and more animal life, more biodiversity. If the car accepts this new role, it will be at the heart of the energy revolution, otherwise it will no longer exist in the future. The car could be an energy tool in a new system of bioenergies. Both in terms of consciousness and empathy, the car is needed because people want to enjoy mobility – they want to go to the beach, move through the landscape, they want to transport things and they want to store and draw upon nature, they want

ENERGY SOURCES IN THE LANDSCAPE OF THE FUTURE

CLOUD 9, © AUDI

ENERGY

01 Wind energy
02 Test Laboratory
03 Bioenergy
04 Offshore wind power
05 Electric mobility
06 Power plants
07 Grid management
08 Energy efficiency
09 Wave energy farms
10 Solar photovoltaic
11 Hydrogen cycle
12 Wind forest
13 Solar thermoelectric
14 Rural microgrids
15 Subestation
16 Urban microgrids
17 Greenpeace Rainbow Warrior

BUILDINGS

A Aviary
B Figueres
C Media-ITC
D La ola
E Santa Monica
F Villa Nurbs

BARCELONA'S EMPATHIC CIVILIZATION
6
10
13
07
11
08
12
E
15
C
16
17
14
F

their car to collect rainwater that one can drink inside it. If the car were empathic with human behavior, all of this could be possible.

So your "Barcelona local car" is not only self-sufficient, but it is also the key to a new energy system on a city scale.
The point is that the buildings of the future will not only consume energy but will also produce energy. If this newly gained energy goes to the grid, we are once again stuck in the old, familiar business where we have to deal with all these lobby aspects. But we could store energy in our car, and at the same time the car could be loaded up with green energy from the house and vice versa. I am not sure if the car will use electricity or if it will be hydrogen-driven, and I don't want to go into the details, because they don't matter in human terms. But in general, in our vision the car is needed to store the energy of the building and it is needed in order to enjoy mobility. Without the car, the system wouldn't be in balance. That's the point.

Will there be individual mobility in your vision or is it going to be replaced by public transport?
I do not think that a clear distinction between public and private transportation will be appropriate in the future. There are so many hybrid possibilities, not only regarding the number of users but also regarding energy sources. More important than the question of public or private is the experience of mobility. And in our case, we envision a car that evidently has many sources of experience: It will host nature, some agriculture and plants.
A vehicle is always an extension of the domestic space, and therefore it is part of your private domain. But at the same time, you can share it publicly. The questions of the future are very much about sharing, networking, chatting and connecting different domains.

Your idea of nature for urban spaces goes much further than just considering green zones. You are interested in the inner functionality of nature, its efficiency and performance. How could we learn from that?
If you think closer to nature, everything is connected. A very small seed, for example, will create a tree that will produce fruits – like a factory of fruits – and with the fruits, other things can be produced, like medicine. The tree then becomes a kind of hospital, a factory for medicine. In the course of a year, we can have more seeds, more trees and more fruits. The whole system expands, grows and gives us oxygen. Have you seen people do anything artificially that was so efficient, productive and generous?

This is where we need to go: To a point where buildings are as generous as those trees, where our cars provide energy and are networking with other cars and with

THUS, WE DON'T WANT TO CHASE THE CARS OUT OF THE CITY, WE WANT THEM TO PLAY A PROMINENT ROLE IN A NEW ENERGY SYSTEM. CONSEQUENTLY, CITIES WILL BE GREENER. WE WILL HAVE MORE NATURE, LESS NEED FOR URBAN SPRAWL. NATURE WILL BE INTEGRATED INTO THE CITY; THE STREETS WILL HAVE ORANGE TREES, AGRICULTURE AND MORE ANIMAL LIFE, MORE BIODIVERSITY. IF THE CAR ACCEPTS THIS NEW ROLE, IT WILL BE AT THE HEART OF THE ENERGY REVOLUTION, OTHERWISE IT WILL NO LONGER EXIST IN THE FUTURE.

houses. Nature takes water from the earth and stores water in the roots and inside of plants. And we, on the contrary, only suck and consume, but we do not store. I suggest an architecture that performs the way that nature does.

Your aim is to create a whole way of life. What is the architect's role in this global view?
As a humanist, the architect has to consider ethics – we've lost a lot of that in our society during the last years. In my eyes, architects must have socio-political aims and visions. Life quality, human resources and empathic behaviour are essential for the architect's work. Business should never be the input; it should always come second.

Sandra Hofmeister, born 1970, is a writer and critic specializing in architecture and design. Following her studies of art history in Berlin, she completed a doctorate in Romance philology in Munich. She has worked for *Deutsche Welle TV* and the editorial offices of *Baumeister* and *Detail*, among others. Her pieces have appeared in such publications as *Mark*, *DAMn°*, *Baumeister* and *Architektur & Wohnen*. Sandra Hofmeister is supporting the Stylepark editorial team with the publications in the context of the *Audi Urban Future Award*.

VIEW OF TOKYO FROM MORI TOWER, ROPPONGI HILLS
PHOTOS: ANTONIA HENSCHEL

LIBERATING THE CITY OR THE JOURNEY IS THE DESTINATION SUBJECTIVE OBSERVATIONS OF A PARTICIPANT IN THE DIALOGUE ON URBAN MOBILITY IN THE FUTURE BY THOMAS WAGNER

001. Charioteering. The desire for self-determined mobility is at least as old as the desire for its mechanical fulfillment. At the turn of the 16th century, court society not only developed central perspective, but also what Jacob Burckhardt described as "mythological and allegorical charioteering"[1] on strangely masked vehicles. The Renaissance trionfo – an allegorical triumphal procession in celebration of not military but ethical or spiritual victories that included all kinds of theatrical machinery – thus imitated divine appearances by way of two tactics: through allegorical masking and through mechanical movement.[2] The gods, in contrast to humans, have always appeared to be independently or auto-mobile, and therefore, in order to feign a likeness to the gods, one needs –and bear this in mind – a vehicle. In other words, even today we consider ourselves gods while driving, if only lesser gods. And floating over the radiator – the art historian Erwin Panofsky identified the precursors of the Rolls-Royce radiator front, which imitates the architecture of a columned portico and evokes the Nike of Samothrace – are the last remnants of the allegorical aesthetics of the trionfo.[3] The delight in automobile movement is a gift from heaven despite the fact that, for as long as humanity has pursued the desire for absolute mobility, it has not only been fixed in its direction but has also contradicted itself with increasing frequency. No trace of free movement – least of all in the city. Are the days of the steering wheel over once and for all; does the "auto" in Autobahn no longer translate to self-determination? Are we on the way to becoming a transport load, caught in a racing standstill?

002. On the road. In this day and age, where things are complex and the journey itself is often declared the only destination, we often hear that it's all about the process. Not that we would lose sight of results – particularly not in the West – but because it has been proven that results are different where there has been cooperation along the way, regardless of where we come from or which ideals, concepts or experiences have shaped us. A process-oriented procedure is thus understood as one in which the progress or development of a project is considered to be a significant part of its success.

From the perspective of the Stylepark team, which has assumed curatorial responsibility for the *Audi Urban Future Award*, the primary objective is for architects and mobility providers like the automobile manufacturer Audi to enter into a constructive dialogue with one another, on visions and concrete concepts as well on the different cultures the respective ideas draw upon. The advantages are obvious: due to the complexity of the task at hand, no one can know how things will evolve or what the future of urban mobility will actually look like in the end, so it is more productive to exchange ideas and arguments than to insist upon one's own, inevitably limited view and to draw conclusions or develop models based on that view alone. In the end, we are all in the same precarious position where the future is concerned: what lies ahead remains unknown and yet every step we take makes the approach of a future present more probable.

003. Intermediate stages. It would have been easy to invite the six participating architects to develop visions or even utopias for the city of the future and the role of mobility without the constraints of the considerably more concrete questions of an automobile manufacturer. Yet that seemed to us to be precisely the wrong way to go about it. And as a result, all participants in the *Audi Urban Future Award* have opened their minds to a collaborative process, in order to become acquainted with and exchange their various ways of thinking and respective approaches and methods with one another. To that extent, what we have decided to call "process" is nothing more than an intermediate stage. No more, but also no less. It initially began with a set of thematic guidelines, a "briefing" that attempted to describe the conceptual scope of the competition in more concrete terms, and was followed by a visit to the Audi facilities in Ingolstadt, an internal workshop at the Design Museum in London and a subsequent public conference at the Royal Institute of British Architects, during which the first concept drafts were presented. The decision to take this indirect route was deliberate and, in my view, it has unquestionably proven to be both unusual and productive. The discussions were always lively and to the point, in spite of the fact that this is a competition, and a competitive situation would usually preclude that kind of exchange. Now that a considerable portion of the journey has been covered, the following picture has taken shape: Where the architects and their presentations are concerned, what happened in Ingolstadt and London could be compared to visiting a group of master chefs the afternoon before a sumptuous feast. Generously, they grant access to their kitchens. The menu and the serving order of the dishes have been determined, the ingredients are on hand for the most part and preparations are underway. Yet what the dishes will look like on the table and, above all, how they will taste, can at best only be imagined.

004. Process logic. As opposed to the logic of planning, which is oriented towards an ideal form that has been designed by intellect and willed to be the goal, the logic of process primarily follows the situation and the continual transformation of things. Therefore the advantage of taking a detour via mutual dialogue lay above all in exploring the whole terrain; each participant paid particular attention to what proved to be fundamental in any given constellation. This kind of approach is effective because it drives things forward by allowing a certain tendency to take shape in the procedure without presupposing a specific model for the results.[4] Trusting in the dialogue and allowing it to follow the drift that develops within the process can change the entire procedure – at least momentarily. Rather than actively pushing a certain perspective, one takes part in the collective achievement of transformation. To go forward on the basis of this type of process thus means to be willing to participate in the adventure of putting one's trust in a form of collective not-knowing.

005. To act or to think. "Life itself," noted Heinrich von Kleist, "is a struggle with Fate; and in our actions it is much as it is in a wrestling match. The wrestler, having hold of his opponent, cannot possibly at that moment proceed otherwise than according to the promptings of the moment; and a man who tried to calculate which muscles he should employ and which limbs he should set in motion in order to win would inevitably be disadvantaged and defeated. But afterwards, when he has won or is lying on the mat, it may be useful and appropriate to think by what application of force he threw his opponent or how he ought to have moved in order to trip him and upright himself. A man must, like that wrestler, take hold of life and feel and sense with a thousand limbs how his opponent twists and turns, resists him, comes at him, evades him and reacts: or he will never get his way in a conversation, much less in a battle."[5]

006. Passing through. We are passing through. We follow a drift, because we want to postpone being confronted with the hard facts a little longer. Or is it just easier for things that are formulated in shadowy and metaphoric terms to sneak past the now widespread pressure to utilize? Processes are not always easy to manage, but the visions of the future can thus escape being crushed by reality, at least for the moment. Doubts remain. Are all of the thoughts attached to unattainable concepts, all of the imaginations and dreams that have yet to find a home and therefore remain u-topic, more than thought bubbles that obscure the sovereign eye like soap bubbles? Or why are "bubbles" suddenly so important? Finding your way around, checking out unfamiliar terrain and giving yourself over to the misunderstandings and pitfalls of an open-ended discussion – all of these things mean navigating changing currents and, in doing so, going down some menacing whitewater rapids every once in a while.

007. Traffic collapse. The reality beyond our debates took its toll regardless. Was it the writing on the wall? The eruption wasn't exactly of Krakatoan proportions, there was no sign of the South Seas or midday heat, no mammoth explosion, no big bang that could be heard thousands of kilometers away. And yet, a magma fire beneath the armor of the geologically instable Icelandic ice wreaked havoc on the entire fabric of European mobility. There was a rupture; the network was torn. Which is why the event also became a – not particularly welcome – part of our work process. In mid-April, nearly four weeks after the sixth-largest Icelandic volcano had become active, the wondrous name of Eyjafjallajökull, which means nothing other than "island-mountain glacier", abruptly became common usage. Westerly winds blew the cloud of volcanic ash made up of minute particles of magma and steam towards Europe. Suddenly, not only a handful of airports in Scandinavia, but all major European traffic hubs were closed and the reality of how vulnerable the global network of our transportation systems really is gradually took hold. On a tiny island – nothing but a whim of nature – a tiny stream of lava emerges from beneath the ice of a glacier and, before you know it, brings the worldwide flow of traffic to a standstill.

008. Down-to-earth. It was Friday, April 16, and we were in Milan, where the world's largest and most important furniture trade fair, the Salone del Mobile, was taking place. And like thousands of others, we were stuck. Nothing but blue sky, not a trace of ash, yet the return flight was cancelled nonetheless. The shocking news making the rounds at the packed main train station was that the next available train to Frankfurt wouldn't be leaving until Sunday evening. By this time, we would of course have to be on our way to London, where the workshop and conference had long been scheduled. After any number of failed attempts to find a rental car, we were finally saved. First in the car of a designer friend and later in a rental, we traversed the Alps and returned to Frankfurt, where we arrived late in the evening. Automobile mobility had, for the moment, triumphed over the traffic net spanning the skies, because it was literally more down-to-earth and more flexible. The memory of the helplessness of immobility suffered will remain. Despite our successful journey homeward, the meetings in London had to be cancelled on Saturday.

009. Early summer night's musing. As I see it, that is also a part of the process or, more precisely, of the beginning of the intensively communicative phase that the competition could now finally enter following the delay caused by the cloud of volcanic ash. I'm in Ingolstadt, where the first meeting of the architects with the Audi engineers, designers, brand and marketing experts is scheduled to take place on Wednesday, May 26 at 11:00. Since the trip from my home takes too long, I arrived the evening before and am now sitting outside the Weissbräuhaus Zum Herrnbräu in the Dollstraße. A nearly full moon is hanging over the rooftops of the old city and the beer is fresh from the tap. At this time of day, there are plenty of pedestrians moving about the historic city center, a few bicyclists, every now and again taxis, busses and a few private cars. At the next table, a couple that may or may not end up together is chatting about Audi, budgets and hood constructions. At the moment, there are no traffic problems in this small Bavarian city. The mobility mix is right on this mild, early summer night.

010. Electrification. It's raining on the morning of May 26. Outside of the hotel, the garbage trucks are rumbling. And in America, so I read, the first affordable electric car is making waves. I ask myself whether people here are also way ahead of politics and companies when it comes to necessary changes? According to *Spiegel Online*, the car – which is manufactured by a Japanese company – will be selling for $32,780 in the United States, and can be had for only $25,280 after a federal tax deduction of $7,500. Residents of California are eligible for another $5,000 from the state and, in the end, they pay less than for a hybrid automobile. Change in the automobile sector is increasingly dynamic. Yet I'm less surprised at the fact that electric drives are becoming ever more common (Audi will also soon be introducing such a car) than I am at the high subsidies that are being offered in America. The defensive nature of the political debates about this type of program being held here in Germany certainly is surprising. But will a different kind of motor really change our cities, too? Summer nights in small cities like Ingolstadt will be even quieter and the air quality will be even better. But nevertheless, I believe we're talking about completely different cities with completely different problems.

011. Don't panic. At breakfast I read Paul Virilio, who is considering the "city of panic": "Better informed about the bottlenecks of Paris than any number of experts, a taxi driver said to me one day: 'Listen mate, if the traffic's bad, it's because the streets are longer than they are wide,' thereby coming out not only on the side of Haussmann against Jules Ferry, but especially letting it be known that the Baron hadn't gone far enough in leveling the place with his roadworks... As though the future of the metropolis was not only the autodrome or the aerodrome, but a return to the desert, to *tabula rasa*!"[6] Is that really possible or is it just a metaphoric coup? Another *tabula rasa*, another round of grand devastation? Will not what the progress critic Virilio calls planetary "incarceration" seek new open spaces somewhere "out of this world" rather than down here on Earth? The anticipation to finally find out what the architects have come up with is mounting. Will there be any worrying, possibly panic-stricken scenarios among them? I calm myself with the thought that it seems to depend on where one decides to look: at the mobile units or at the territory in which they move.

012. Future on the test stand. Not much later, at the Audi facilities, such thoughts are long gone. From here on, it's all about themes like "Efficiency, Emotion, Connectivity and Architecture", whereby the term architecture doesn't refer to a building, but rather to the structure of an automobile. Whether in a driving simulator for testing the interface between car and driver – which has to function and which the customer has to like and feel comfortable with – or a spectacular crash test, wherever future developments are the subject of discussion, it's always about first improving what exists. The future appears in the form of an optimized present. Which, in light of the technical attention that is paid to every detail here, translates into a tremendous effort. We learn about the precision with which new safety systems combine passive and active safety and how important it is to continue to develop not only the car but also the infrastructure. In all likelihood, cars will soon not only be equipped with adaptive cruise control systems and attention-monitoring assistant systems, but will also be able to "see and hear", in other words, to communicate with one another.

ARCHITECTS VISITING INGOLSTADT
PHOTOS: SABINE REITMAIER, © AUDI

013. Optimized present. As nice as all of that may seem, don't human beings come across as defective creatures that can only retain their mobility with highly developed technical crutches? Where are we headed? To the auto-elimination of the automobile as a manually operated system? Technically, the future lies in networking, in assisted systems, in greater safety and improved quality. There can be no doubt about that. What will come will be situated somewhere between the old motorcar and a fully automated system. It will be integrated and hybrid. That the future will be driven by electricity is also a done deal. Not only in order to reduce CO_2 emissions, and certainly not as a stripped-down variety of transport, but rather with "power, emotion and passion" so that fun, economy and responsibility can be united under one car roof.

But it is also clear that, for a globally active company like Audi, there has to be more than one future. Like it or not, they will need many of them, and so development is focused on not just one kind of ideal vision tailored to only one market, but on the needs of very different parts of the world. It doesn't make it any easier that an average of four to five years go into the development of a finished product from an initial sketch. And what if the future looks different in the meantime? At any rate, the Audi designers impressively demonstrate what makes an Audi look and feel like an Audi. Will that change, someone asks? Which role will the aesthetics of efficiency play in the coming years? That remains to be seen. A discussion about the Audi A2 reveals that it's not all that easy for a company when it has to be ahead of its time. A consensus is quickly reached: a wonderful vehicle with great potential that was unfortunately not honored by the market. The early bird is punished by the customer – that, too, says something about how difficult it can be to deal with the future. Especially when society is rapidly changing and one wants to hold onto the role of an "ambassador of change". This much is clear: in the future, progress – Vorsprung – will be defined to a much greater extent by efficiency and sustainability.

014. Transfer. Early in the morning the following day, we fly back to London. There is the usual congestion on the way from Heathrow to the Design Museum. In the back of a spacious Audi A8 limousine, time passes pleasantly with discussions of the previous day. With a slight delay, Heinrich Wefing greets the participants. The workshop begins. The skies are gray, but the walls are blue.

015. From A to B. Now down to business. The presentations of the initial concepts begin, in alphabetical order, with Alison Brooks of ABA. It's about "Convergence and Diffusion", about things that are drifting apart and need to be brought back together: the city, nature, quality of life and transportation, and all of that after the flowery dreams of the so-called "Space Age" with its flying cars. Oriented towards the common good, Alison Brooks asks how social interaction can be expressed in architectural and social terms. One of her demands is that cars should be smaller, maybe even small enough to be taken into the apartment. Urban space must also be reallocated, resulting in a "microcar city" in which a car can be shared with the neighbors or temporarily integrated into the home as a "plug in". Perhaps that will soon be the greatest luxury: to own a car and to be able to afford to use it.

Bjarke Ingels of BIG is next, and he immediately steps up the tempo, at least where word flow is concerned. What he's driven by, and what he describes based on his design for the Danish Pavilion for the Expo in Shanghai, are the various flows and currents into which the movements of a mass are organized. Mass and congestion should be regulated with minimal restrictions, so that the movements of all road users can flow as freely as possible. Information technology and automated, driverless driving play a significant role. But does the swarm really move more intelligently than the individual does? Or is that just another illusion?

016. Empathy. Enric Ruiz-Geli of Cloud 9 takes a very different approach, not only because he put the question about the car of the future to children who will be 28 to 30 years old in 20 years. The example that he presents in a short film is certainly very charming: A car that consists of Scotch tape rolls and thousands of tiny air bubbles and of air, and is driven by nothing but a breath of air – a truly pneumatic vehicle. What Ruiz-Geli has in mind is a civilization that is based not only on technology, but also on empathy and, because it is not merely geopolitically but biopolitically oriented, places greater importance on local factors and atmospheres. From which he grandiosely yet somewhat naively concludes that a car must also adapt to local conditions, for example, in Barcelona it wouldn't need a heating system. Even if his "Barcelona Empathic Car" never becomes more than a nice metaphor for a different way of thinking, its empathic and osmotic air design is stimulating all the same because, in this age of global bubbles, it calls for a proximity to things that would change fundamental attitudes towards the environment. Ruiz-Geli is not betting on a digital network, which will be gone with the wind because we will take its place ourselves by turning to face the world in empathy.

017. Mobile population. At first glance, the concept of New York architects Diller Scofidio + Renfro, presented in London by David Allin, seemed simple enough. If the mobile population is growing, with people in mobile homes – at least in America – constantly moving from one place to the next, then the question arises as to which consequences result from the development of such dynamic communities. In what relationship do they stand to those who prefer to statically dwell in one place? Can the two perhaps be combined? This initial sketch also contains a charming provocation along the lines of: this is how the utopia game is played, so this is how we're playing it and we're presenting the future of the past as a kind of redesign of the concept of the Plug-in-City proposed by the Archigram planners nearly fifty years ago. The subtext seems to be that we no longer have urban utopias today. Pursue them anyway, and you'll automatically be thrown back in time and will find yourself in the 1960s. It will be interesting to see how it evolves in the end in Venice.

018. Mobile home. Who knows, maybe there really is a big chunk of the future behind the combination of driving and living. "Mobile home owners", as the philosopher Vilém Flusser explains, "are not nomads, because they move around in pursuit of neither buffalo nor chickens, but rather in search of "pure reason". Camping as a social system therefore represents not a tribe, but rather a lonely and randomly composed mass."[7] All the same, the motor home – an "artificial belly" that rolls over its own foundation – is a good thing for the "new man of tomorrow". As yet, according to Flusser, apartments and homes have not been completely outpaced by the mobile home, a lifestyle that is restricted to leisure time and place because the place and time-specific nature of work imposes itself upon everything else. But that could change, should the tendency towards reduced working hours persist. At some point, quantity would become quality and then, in the words of the Holy Scriptures, "a trumpet will sound and we will all be transformed": into mobile home owners.

019. Harmony. Resolutely, Jürgen Mayer H. set his stakes on network-assisted, automated driving in the inner city. What motivates him are the new possibilities for perception and body experience that such systems imply. Not only would the automated flow of traffic create new scope and room for possibility in the city, but based on the enormous capacity of traffic control, the urban area could be cleansed of unnecessary ballast, as if by running it through a digital carwash. Whether the resulting fuzziness will really lead to new freedoms or even to a completely individualized perception of the city seems to be less probable than that cities will, in the future, experience inward expansion.

ROYAL INSTITUTE OF BRITISH ARCHITECTS IN LONDON
PHOTOS: SABINE REITMAIER, © AUDI

ROYAL INSTITUTE OF BRITISH ARCHITECT
66
6
RIBA

Whereas Jürgen Mayer H. was aiming for harmony in the relationship between mobility and buildings, Zhang Ke of Standardarchitecture put forward a mixture of growth criticism, optimism and revolutionary irony united in a vision entitled "Harmonious Beijing". In China, as he made clear, clocks tick differently: under the enormous pressure of rural exodus and population growth, the transformation of cities is not progressing at a leisurely evolutionary pace, but rather in the form of permanent, revolutionary upheaval. What was new yesterday is already gone today. But a new, "moving ring" built around the inner city, which sprawls out through a series of rings, might help: a new form of "moving city" that takes shape above a ring of metro lines organized horizontally and vertically around the existing infrastructure, with gigantic green conical structures towering above the ring, all of them connected to the underground network. Add the movement of a conveyor belt and the city opens itself up to public life on the endless belt of constantly moving streets. A realistic response where the analysis of the problem is concerned, yet the proposed solutions are tinged by irony. Thus did the sun of the new collective rise in the East, grounded by the deceptive pathos of Chinese revolutionary opera.

020. Bubbles. It seems that speaking of bubbles, spheres and capsules has never been so timely or epidemic. Yet, in spite of all the economic bubbles that – at least metaphorically speaking – have burst in recent years, these enclosures and encapsulations are generally seen in a positive light. Has isolation shed its fright factor? Are we readying ourselves for a future of living and traveling in climate capsules and individualized bubbles? Whether microcar, air bubble, chain of bubbles or soap bubbles, imaginations everywhere are attached to bubbles, to these, as the philosopher Peter Sloterdijk calls them in the first volume of his *Spheres* trilogy, "intimate forms of rounded being-in-form". [8] Will these new time and space capsules have openings, communicative interfaces and network synapses, so that their inmates can maintain a connection to the larger web? Or are such fantasies merely metaphors for a wistful and momentarily therapeutic return to the womb?

021. Conference. Friday, May 28. The sun is shining in London and the Golden Eagle pub on the corner of Marylebone Lane has made it through the night in one piece. Not a trace of a traffic jam or a city in panic. Some people are out buying bread, others are on their way to work; the neighborhood feels nearly idyllic. A few blocks away at the Royal Institute of British Architects, the room is slowly filling up. Rupert Stadler, the CEO of Audi AG, is explaining what the project is essentially about: "We are thinking in the long term; not only are we an automobile manufacturer, but to a certain extent we're also a mobility provider and, in the future, we'll be answering many more questions than we have up to now." Subsequently, all positions and interim results are presented to the public and put up for discussion. Some think there is too much focus on the car and too little on the city. As the music of the Chinese revolutionary opera floods the room, no one notices that the Embassy of the People's Republic of China to Great Britain is only a stone's throw away, just across from the Royal Institute of British Architects. There was no word of a protest demarche.

022. Perspectives. Will we be at home in motion in the future? Will the static architectural properties of a house be aligned with those of an audio-visually equipped vehicle; will home and car simultaneously become both intelligent and interactive? Will we soon live anywhere and will the car – not exclusively, but additionally – become a kind of furniture, as Paul Virilio predicts? It is clear that we are stuck in the middle and there is no end to the questions. After the Earth and the air, will our sight now be conquered? Will the blue planet become one big congested suburb, or will we be removed from the physical reality, surfing the cybernetic ether?

When Richard Hamilton, the father of British Pop Art, made his famous collage "Just what is it that makes today's homes so different, so appealing?" for the 1956 interdisciplinary exhibition "This is Tomorrow" at the Whitechapel Gallery in London, the apartment had long since ceased to be an isolated, self-contained shell, but was rather shaped by diverse appliances and media. At the center of Hamilton's collage is a man (Adam) who has sculpted his body and put it on display to the same extent as the pin-up girl (Eve), who is posing and presenting herself as a commodity. The bodybuilder is holding a lollipop in his hand, which carries the brand name "POP" on its wrapper.[9] All media exist alongside one another and are permanently accessible: painting, comics, newspapers, cinema, poster, television and audio. The space is open-plan and extends itself over several levels, has big windows and, floating in space above the open roof of the scene, is the planet Earth. Vacuum cleaner, philodendron and canned ham are represented as well as a patterned carpet that is actually the image of a beach scene blown up to the point of abstraction. And the lampshade flaunts the Ford logo. Hamilton has said that he was intent on incorporating all of the objects and ideas that preoccupied the post-war consciousness in his collage.[10] And he continues: by all indications, things appeared to be moving towards a promising future and there seemed to be no limit to the technological advancements taking place. Nevertheless, as Hamilton explained, despite the wave of optimism that carried society into the 1960's, some of the furnishings in his intérieur convey a feeling of wariness.[11] In the updated version of Hamilton's interior presented by Alison Brooks today, the automobile as a roommate is admittedly not the only addition. In one respect, the perspective has been fundamentally changed: the eye no longer perceives heaven opening up to the planet Earth, the ceiling is now open to the blue sky.

023. Everything is in flux. Process, as was again and again made clear during the discussions, translates to: "I have no knowledge of these things, but I am capable of listening and observing closely, understanding and learning." Or in other words, it means cooperation instead of "I told you so." The initial concepts have now been presented and discussed. Nothing is yet final; much is in flux. It is only initially surprising that – much to the amazement of all those who spend their days developing and building cars – all of the architects participating in the competition gave first consideration to "charioteering" and the requisite vehicle. Architects know a lot about buildings and urban structures, but less about cars. Here, there are a few things they can learn; they can become familiar with perspectives that will not be without consequences for their own work.
Of that, we are certain. And from this point on, we are all of us – the architects, Audi representatives and the Stylepark team – on the road to Venice.

[1] J. Burckhardt, *The Culture of the Renaissance in Italy*, transl. S.G.C. Middlemore (London, 1878) p. 197.

[2] See J. J. Berns, *Die Herkunft des Automobils aus Himmelstrionfo und Höllenmaschine* (Berlin, 1996).

[3] E. Panofsky, *"The Ideological Antecedents of the Rolls-Royce Radiator"* in: *Three Essays on Style*, ed. I. Lavin (London, 1995).

[4] See F. Julien, *Der Umweg über China. Ein Ortswechsel des Denkens* (Berlin, 2002) p. 48.

[5] Heinrich von Kleist, *"Reflection. A Paradox"* in *Selected Writings* by Heinrich von Kleist, ed. and transl. D. Constantine (Indianapolis, 2004) p. 410.

[6] P. Virilio, *City of Panic*, transl. J. Rose (Oxford & New York, 2007) p. 13.

[7] V. Flusser, *"Wohnwagen"*, in *Von der Freiheit des Migranten*, Einsprüche gegen den Nationalismus (Berlin, 2000) p 45–49.

[8] P. Sloterdijk, *Sphären*, Bd. 1: *Blasen* (Frankfurt a. M., 1998) p. 63.

[9] R. Hamilton, *Malen nach Zahlen* (London & Bangkok, 2006) p. 15.

[10] R. Hamilton, *"Ein Blick von Innen"*, in *Exteriors, Interiors, Objects, People*, ed. R. Hamilton (exh. cat. Winterthur, Hanover & Valencia, 1991) p. 138.

[11] R. Hamilton, *"Ein Blick von Innen"*, p. 138.

Thomas Wagner is a member of the Stylepark editorial team and is a contributor to the conception of the *Audi Urban Future Award*. From 1991 to 2007, he was editor for art and design at the *Frankfurter Allgemeine Zeitung*, and today he works as a freelance writer and art critic. He is an honorary professor at the Academy of Fine Arts in Nuremberg and recently published the volume *Licht im Schacht von Babel*, including texts on the documenta in Kassel and the Art Biennale in Venice.

DESIGN MUSEUM IN LONDON
PHOTOS: SABINE REITMAIER, © AUDI

THE AUDI PERSPECTIVE ON THE FUTURE OF THE AUTOMOBILE

The Audi Think Tank is an internal panel that was founded specifically for the purpose of interacting with the architects throughout the course of the *Audi Urban Future Award*. The idea was that the competition should not simply be carried out parallel to the developments and concepts at Audi, but that from the very beginning it should be conceived as a dialogue between the selected architects and the representatives of individual Audi divisions.

The "think tank" concept has a long-standing tradition at Audi. In the past, various bodies have often been formed to reflect upon the future, independently of concrete objectives and free of all internal constraints. This kind of reflection on future developments has been taken to a new dimension with the Audi Think Tank for the *Audi Urban Future Award*. Together with Stylepark, Audi colleagues are now engaged in a discussion on themes and methods that are derived from completely different perspectives – first and foremost from the perspective of architects. Both sides stand to learn a great deal from one another in this process.

The members of the Audi Think Tank are Antje Bauer (Communication), Christian Labonte (Design Strategy and Communication), Annegret Maier (Brand Strategy), Thomas Müller (Technical Development Strategy), Bernhard Neumann (Event Marketing) and Dominik Stampfl (Corporate Strategy). The committee will remain intact during in the intervals between competitions, in order to reflect upon the results of the *Audi Urban Future Award* and their consequences.

From the perspective of the Audi Think Tank, there are three fields of primary relevance in an open discussion with architects and urban planners on the future of inner-city mobility: the future brand strategy, current technological developments and aesthetic parameters in a broader sense or, in other words, decisions with regard to design.

BRAND STRATEGY

Where the identity of the Audi brand is concerned, the following question might be posed: What distinguishes Audi from other automobile manufacturers both today and in the future? Of the three European premium manufacturers, Audi can look back upon the most recent success story. Within the past twenty years Audi has gained lots of ground and today is one of the strongest competitors in the so-called premium segment. Nevertheless, Audi's history goes back much further. And one theme can be identified that runs like a thread through its entire, over one-hundred-year history: the courage to do things differently, to break with conventions and to set new standards, while always remaining down-to-earth.

Audi has always had the sympathies of the customer on its side, even though the company hasn't always staked a full claim as a premium brand. Why is that? Because the modern, young or young-at-heart customer of today no longer wants to submit to a stereotype. The brand is benefiting from this development at a time when classic status symbols are clearly losing their relevance. Audi can thus create an authentic future and meet the oncoming requirements of premium customers, if not already anticipate them, because the values that define the brand complement its drivers rather than patronizing them or encumbering them with an image that they don't actually identify with.

Audi is not a brand that, like a status symbol, stands above the driver and outshines his or her personality. On the contrary, Audi considers itself a partner to a user who is committed to performance in a congenial form. Here, a certain degree of understatement plays a role, as well as the company's conviction that customer and manufacturer must be on equal footing. Owning an automobile is at least to some extent an expression of individual personality, a fact that is sure to retain its relevance in the future as well.

What will continue to change in the coming years is the concept of "premium". As opposed to luxury, premium stands for a real and objectively quantifiable value added for the customer. While this value added was previously substantiated in factual or tangible aspects like technical features and safety features, among others, today we are moving more and more towards aspects of an emotional nature, which are difficult to classify, such as services relating to all aspects of the product that can make life easier for the client in a variety of ways. For example, a "real relationship" in which a salesperson becomes a trusted partner may prove to be the key to a successful future, particularly in the event that the ratio between owners and users continues to shift.

The relationship to the car as an individually configured place of retreat, which one can "furnish" according to one's own tastes and personal preferences, is becoming more important. The way in which the relationship to a vehicle, in the sense of an absolutely reliable "partner" in individual mobility and a guarantor of freedom and self-determination, can be newly defined will be essential. In this context, Audi is considering complementary mobility services that would offer the customer value added above and beyond individual car ownership. In conjunction with our standards as a premium manufacturer, such aspects as lavish and innovative interior concepts or timesaving services are gaining significance. Individual mobility will thus become more closely associated with the feeling of being able to strip off the hectic side of everyday life and escape the pressure for a moment, because one feels not only secure in a vehicle, but also comfortable as one can listen to music, talk on the phone or work there.

The Audi brand can accomplish all of these things in an authentic way, especially if – building on the roots of the brand and the success of recent years – those qualities that characterize Audi and have enabled it to create what we consider "automobile premium" are taken into account: continually forging new paths and setting technological standards, true to the slogan "Vorsprung durch Technik". After all, winning over our customers with understatement, generosity, charming provocation and a design that leaves its mark on the style of the times will continue to be the goal in the future.

In this context, sustainability is not a singular and most certainly not an isolated subject. On the contrary, the continual optimization of processes and products, offering our customers superior solutions at all times and thus actively shaping the future, corresponds to Audi's concept of itself as a company. For us as a brand, sustainability in its fundamental definition as "an effect that is sustained over a long period of time" means: to consider at all times the consequences of personal and corporate actions, not to pursue short-lived trends but to adopt a long-term approach to themes and give them substance, so that we can continue to provide the customer with sound arguments in favor of a premium product. Therefore, such aspects are central to all deliberations of future projects and products.

TECHNOLOGY

"Vorsprung durch Technik" is more than just a slogan for Audi. The concept of Vorsprung – or progress – runs like a thread through all of the company's technological developments, and is by no means restricted to components and systems. More than anything else, the integration of all systems and the complex field of networking will play an important role in the technological development process in the years to come. Whereas the focus during the last decade was on the concept of interconnecting systems within the automobile, in the next ten years networking will be extended beyond the vehicle. In other words, in the future the vehicle will communicate with its environment and with other automobiles. As a result, networking will give rise to innovative functions that add fun for the customer and make mobility even more comfortable and secure.

The customers of tomorrow are constantly interlinked via mobile technology and so-called "social media" like Twitter or Facebook. In order to be able to react to these new requirements in the future, the social environment and the automobile environment must be integrated, or merged into one. For example, it is becoming increasingly important to be able to be online at all times, even in an automobile, to have access to search engines, databases and individual networks or to find information about services and infrastructure such as filling stations. This trend was taken up in the new Audi A8, the first automobile to be equipped with – in addition to a navigation system – a wi-fi hotspot that can accommodate up to eight devices at a time.

A significant advantage of this type of "Car2x" communication between the car and the infrastructure will be improved traffic flow. In this context, the "Travolution" project represents a step towards the future. In collaboration with its project partners, Audi has developed an algorithm for the optimization of traffic-light control. Internet-based software influences the entire network of traffic-lights in order to keep waiting times to a minimum and reduce automobile consumption. The second step is of even greater interest: traffic lights will be equipped with communication modules that send the timing of the next green phase to the car's onboard computer. The infotainment system then indicates to the driver the speed at which he or she should drive in order to pass through the traffic light without stopping. This would conserve 700,000 liters of gas per year in Ingolstadt alone and, more importantly, would allow for a more relaxed and improved traffic flow, also resulting in increased safety in inner-city traffic: a basis for sustainable mobility.

Not only networking the automobile with various services, but also communication between individual cars is a relevant aspect of the concept of Vorsprung. In the context of "Car2Car" communication, the exchange of traffic and positioning data between individual vehicles can help to avoid accidents.

The global increase in traffic not only has consequences for people but also for the environment. As an automobile manufacturer Audi therefore carries responsibility for creating a sustainable future. In our strategy, electrification plays a significant role. Audi has already adopted a clear position with the e-tron and, from the sports car to the A1 Mega City Vehicle, has given its dedication to electromobility a face.

DESIGN

When it comes to defining "premium" in the context of the automobility of the future, the first question from the perspective of the designer must be: What will a premium vehicle's value added consist of in the future? In the years to come, what will distinguish a premium model from a standard vehicle? Or, to put it differently, which aspects of usability will become more "humane"? Which solutions will prove to be not only more intelligent, but also more sustainable?

Communication and networking once again take to the foreground in finding answers to these questions from the perspective of the designer. In concrete terms, this means that designers will need to consider both communication between automobiles (Car2Car) and communication between car and infrastructure (Car2x), for example, between pedestrians at crosswalks and approaching vehicles. It will be important to take customer needs in this area into account and to develop new solutions for interior architecture, possibly even completely new vehicle concepts.

Where interior design is concerned, future solutions will primarily be enabled by the implementation of innovative technologies at the interface between man and machine: many technologies are already available, including assisted systems culminating in automated driving, head-up displays and drive-by-wire technology that allows one to steer, shift, accelerate and brake without mechanical linkages.

Where there is a demand for innovative design solutions, the Car2Car and Car2x interfaces present a particular challenge.

IN THE FUTURE THE VEHICLE WILL COMMUNICATE WITH ITS ENVIRONMENT AND WITH OTHER AUTO-MOBILES. AS A RESULT, NETWORKING WILL GIVE RISE TO INNOVATIVE FUNCTIONS THAT ADD FUN FOR THE CUSTOMER AND MAKE MOBILITY EVEN MORE COMFORTABLE AND SECURE.

The many already existing networks can be used to support these interactions, but the integration of the interfaces into the vehicle requires a particularly user-friendly design. Interfaces for personal mobile devices such as smart phones will soon be standard in the form of simple, plug-in solutions.

From the perspective of the automobile designer, a progressive "de-mechanization" of the car serves one principal objective: it creates more leeway for design. Where new construction methods and lightweight materials make a new kind of intelligent lightweight construction possible, the designer is provided with an opportunity to develop new and progressive interior concepts. In the years to come, one of the principal tasks will be to translate these concepts into concrete interior products. Our vehicle interiors will be increasingly characterized by a feeling of lightness and openness. The consolidation of control panels allows for the creation of entirely new and surprising cockpits. These developments are intended to enable the customer to interact with the vehicle in a highly intuitive manner. Because these systems also increase driver and passenger safety, they make it possible to emotionally intensify the driving experience through a more creative presentation of information than previously possible. The possibilities range from new options for entertainment while sitting in traffic to mobile office solutions for working comfortably and effectively while on the road.

New engine systems create room for new possibilities not only technically but also aesthetically, in terms of the car's "architecture" and proportions. What are the specific degrees of freedom? The entire automobile industry is in the middle of a fundamental transformation comparable to the transition from the steam locomotive to an electric locomotive. Accompanying this transformation is a spirit of innovative optimism that boosts creativity. Suddenly, there are any number of new design options. The discontinuation of the so-called

FROM THE PERSPECTIVE OF THE AUTOMOBILE DESIGNER, A PROGRESSIVE "DE-MECHANIZATION" OF THE CAR SERVES ONE PRINCIPAL OBJECTIVE: IT CREATES MORE LEEWAY FOR DESIGN. WHERE NEW CONSTRUCTION METHODS AND LIGHTWEIGHT MATERIALS MAKE A NEW KIND OF INTELLIGENT LIGHTWEIGHT CONSTRUCTION POSSIBLE, THE DESIGNER IS PROVIDED WITH AN OPPORTUNITY TO DEVELOP NEW AND PROGRESSIVE INTERIOR CONCEPTS. IN THE YEARS TO COME, ONE OF THE PRINCIPAL TASKS WILL BE TO TRANSLATE THESE CONCEPTS INTO CONCRETE INTERIOR PRODUCTS.

"powertrain", which includes the vehicle's engine, transmission, driveshafts, differentials and the final drive, allows for the realization of completely different and innovative vehicle layouts.

As a premium brand, Audi generally tends toward an evolutionary approach, setting individual revolutionary milestones along the way. As opposed to hybrid drive system technologies, which represent only an interim solution from a technological perspective, the purely electric drive system is a real innovation. Its distinct nature must be reinterpreted aesthetically. New semantic coding in the product design will be developed, that is, there will be a logical connection between form and content. In other words, the customer should be able to recognize immediately that this is a vehicle with a different drive system. The design features of our e-tron concept vehicle display initial steps, including matrix beam headlight modules, a grille that opens ventilation flaps only as needed and distinct openings for air intake to the battery space whose form is determined by their function.

Today's Audi is sporty, elegant and conveys a feeling of prestige; in that spirit, it can be referred to as classic and emotional. An electric-drive Audi will be intelligent and clever as well, and as such could be classified as progressive and emotional. Electric-drive cars are the appropriate response to the needs of users who travel in urban environments, navigating primarily short distances. With the development of electric-drive cars, there are many parameters to be considered. For example, cabin configuration with its classic seating arrangement could be changed because short-distance urban drivers don't necessarily need four full seats. Vehicle overhangs could be reduced, and slower speeds in the city would reduce aerodynamic requirements for the vehicle body so that taller vehicles could be built. Even the hood would be obsolete so that the front end of a two-box vehicle could be shortened significantly. All of these options for impending changes give us the opportunity today to develop new, genuine automobile archetypes, vehicles with milestone character like the Audi TT or the Audi A7.

www.audi.com

DILLER SCOFIDIO + RENFRO

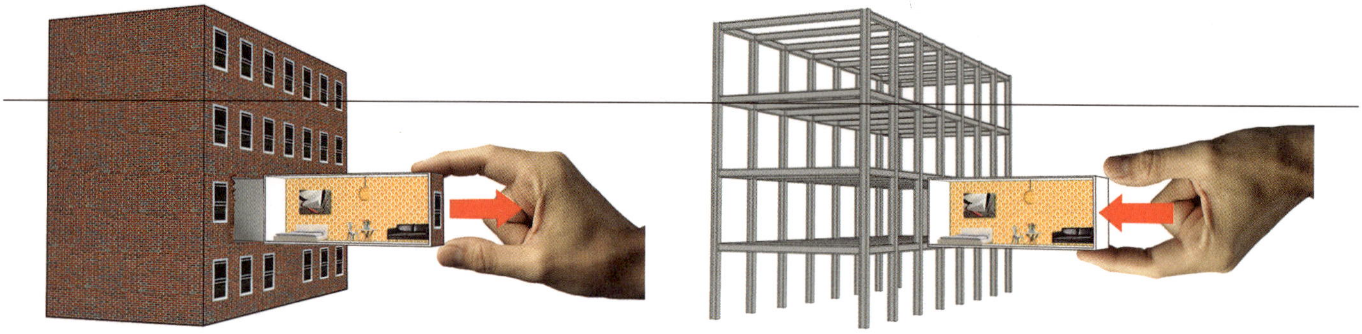

PRESENTATION DILLER SCOFIDIO + RENFRO
DILLER SCOFIDIO + RENFRO, © AUDI

MOBILE UNITS

While cities evolve slowly, the social and professional networks within them are no longer tied to their geography and therefore have become increasingly fluid and fast. Telecommunication technologies and online social networking allow community building without neighborhoods, and presence without proximity. While future visions at the turn of the 21st century predicted population dispersal and teleconferencing replacing commuting, cities are getting denser and people continue to enjoy being next to each other. The city of the future must accommodate these dual tendencies and be simultaneously fast and slow, global and local.

However, it is an inevitable paradox that visions of the future are both a product of the present and are subject to immediate obsolescence. Rather than offering a singular solution to the problems of today, we propose a fuzzy picture of possible future cities enacted by the experimentation of social groups, and enabled by rethinking mobility at the irreducible urban unit of the dwelling.

Instead of a slow city with fast transportation, we imagine a fast city with slow transportation. Slow transportation is already a reality in many large cities, as the car has become increasingly ineffective as a means of moving large numbers of people within a small area. Covering an average of 9.4 square meters, the car is almost half the size of the average personal living space in urban China, and traveling at an average speed of 1.7 miles per hour in Midtown Manhattan, it is outpaced by simply walking. Rather than responding by adding more lanes of traffic, cities like New York City and London have begun replacing lanes with bike paths and urban parks. Given these trends, along with shrinking city budgets and the enormous costs of large-scale public transportation systems, it is not unrealistic to imagine a future city with walking as the primary means of transportation.

Yet if local transportation slows down, personal mobility must speed up so people can live where they want to be and move at a moment's notice. From young professionals who need to frequently relocate in order to work, to retirees with a newfound freedom, the public has many reasons to be in motion. This project imagines a system and components for a mobile domestic space to accommodate that movement. The mobile unit, a detachable and moveable living unit, is self-sufficient and able to connect into a larger network. It contains a person's personal space that always remains intact. Three components – the actual living unit, a vehicle that is used to transport and supply the unit with services, and a secondary structure that holds, organizes and services multiple units – work together to allow an individual an alternative to hotels, extended stays and moving boxes.

When the mobile unit arrives at a new urban area, a secondary structure determines the organization of the units in relationship to each other and the city. It can vary from a dense steel frame that stacks units with connections for water, sewage and power to ramps that allow one unit to back onto the top of another. The design of the secondary structure facilitates the urban community within the context of the city. The vehicle provides sustainable ways of producing water and electricity, which allows the unit to be self-sustaining for an indefinite amount of time, or to be tied into urban infrastructure systems as a consumer or producer.

The following are a few possibilities of how the mobile unit could be deployed to produce new city types and support a range of lifestyles:

ROGUE URBANISM

Although streets occupy a significant portion of open urban space, moving traffic has cordoned off functioning streets to pedestrians in almost all scenarios. The car, with all its appeal as a private amenity, occupies an uncomfortable but culturally accepted area on public streets. If some of the streetscape were given back to the people, openings on the street could function like parking spaces for the mobile unit. Pre-selected, metered spots would give order to the system, and alternate available locations would encourage people to move at regular intervals. Aside from the occasional illegal parker, a person's opportunity to move to their favorite neighborhood would, through a pre-selection system, depend on who is leaving and when.

POP-UP TEMPORARY

The combination of collective interest and the Internet are generating virtual communities for nearly everything. These interests can often be extremely local and specific to one place and, with social networking platforms, they are more easily formed between people anywhere in the world. Interest groups have exploded into instant mega-cities with certain events like Burning Man and the annual Quartzsite RV convention, which bring millions of people together. These places often live year-round off of the income generated from a week of events, yet they do not have the facilities for fluctuating urban-scale populations. The mobile unit facilitates face-to-face connections of similar interest groups by allowing them to bring their unit and create functioning and instant temporary cities.

CUT AND PASTE FAMILY

Patchwork families have begun occupying a greater number of homes in recent years. Increasing numbers of divorces, aging parents, and children who move back home have ruptured the stereotype of two kids and a dog. The situation at home has become infinitely more complicated, not just for families but also for the houses in which they live. The mobile unit offers a solution for these families, without requiring them to give up their homes or surrender personal space. Family members returning home have the ability to bring their own space with them without infringing on the space of the others. And, if they like, they are given the added benefit of being decidedly temporary.

THE LAST "LAST FRONTIER"

Traffic jams, faster modes of transport and the increasing costs of maintaining a car have taken the allure out of the open road. Rather than maintaining itself as an adventurous way of traveling, the car has become a mundane machine responsible for getting people from point A to point B. However, as the dynamics of the Earth change, transport across the Arctic is becoming possible and connections across the northern hemisphere are becoming drivable. The sustainability of the mobile unit as a self-contained, energy- and water-producing unit allows people to venture out on these treks and return to a pioneering sensibility as originally engendered by the automobile.

Diller Scofidio + Renfro

www.dillerscofidio.com

PRESENTATION DILLER SCOFIDIO + RENFRO
DILLER SCOFIDIO + RENFRO, © AUDI

WHEN APARTMENTS TRAVEL

RICARDO SCOFIDIO INTERVIEWED BY JÖRG HÄNTZSCHEL IN NEW YORK

Within the space of only a few years, New York-based Diller, Scofidio and Renfro, founded by husband and wife Elizabeth Diller and Ricardo Scofidio, has become one of the world's most influential architectural firms. With their cerebral yet accessible designs, they remain loyal to the Modernist ethos yet replace monumentalism and pathos with transparency and playfulness. The same holds true for the architects' vision of traveling homes that would be able to cross borders and break down barriers as a reaction to the needs of life in the future.

Mr. Scofidio, you and your wife started your firm three decades ago, but until recently hardly any of your buildings were built.
We did performance pieces, theater, public art. We didn't have a client, we didn't have a sponsor. We got into debt with credit cards, we got some funding from art organizations. But basically we were our own clients.

And you preferred it that way?
We started in 1979, in the middle of a recession. A lot of architects went to galleries and sold their drawings. We wanted to build. We wanted to make things in space. I was also very unhappy with the profession – not with the discipline, but with the profession. It focused on "being a service to…". So I think we were able to be much more exploratory in those early projects. Because once you have a client, you have a budget; you have restrictions and you don't have the same freedom as when you're autonomous and independent. But we never considered ourselves artists. We were looking at the world through the eyes of architects, not artists.

Do you continue to work on these smaller, interdisciplinary projects?
Absolutely. It's critical. We have what we call our "money-losing division" in the office. We did a project which is traveling now for the Fondation Cartier in Paris, we did a piece in Italy on prisons, we are doing a performance piece in New York City. That's part of who we are, we couldn't stop doing that.

How did your breakthrough come about?
I don't know. We didn't change. We had a house that didn't get built, called the Slow House in Long Island. We built the foundation, but the client ran out of money. Probably the biggest thing that happened was when the Institute of Contemporary Art in Boston hired us to do their new building.

With the High Line and the renovation of Lincoln Center in New York, an extension for the Hirshhorn Museum in Washington and a museum in Rio in the works, you have quickly become specialists in public buildings.
Elizabeth and I have researched this area for many years. We have looked into social conventions, the relationship of people and public space and the idea of performance. We've invested in a number of things from domesticity to mass public events.

One of the things that stand out about your buildings is a certain narrative quality. You could almost call them entertaining. Something new happens on every corner.
Architects tend to abstract things. It comes with the architectural education. You're making drawings, you make models, you're continuously abstracting. As a result, when architects start working in the world they tend not to be inclusive but exclusive. We like to be very inclusive and bring everything in. We don't look at the site as a tabula rasa. We see it as loaded with history, social interaction and other factors. I think that creates a narrative structure automatically. We're not formalists.

Let's take the example of Lincoln Center, your biggest project so far.
There are some incredibly good things about it, but at the same time the architects and planners who built it 50 years ago kept the city out because they hated it. It is an acropolis with walls. It was a bad neighborhood at the time. There were people there they didn't want. We were hired, I think, because we wanted to

RICARDO SCOFIDIO AND JÖRG HÄNTZSCHEL
PHOTO: BJÖRN WALLANDER, © AUDI

make Lincoln Center more Lincoln Center than Lincoln Center. Many of the other architects in the competition said, "This place is terrible, tear it down! Let's build over!" We wanted to reveal what it is, who is there and how it is used. Do a striptease. Remove a lot of the travertine and open it up to the public. We wanted to make a place where you would like to hang out, where you would feel you're part of what's going on in the city.

There are sloping lawns, lit walkways, a little amphitheater. It feels a little bit like a playground for dressed-up people.
We want everybody to feel like an actor on a stage. I remember the first time I was in Paris and went to the Garnier Opera. You sit there and you're enjoying the performance, and then there's an intermission. But you don't walk out into some boring lobby, you come out onto a grand stage, and suddenly everybody is a performer. The change in people is immediately visible: the way they stand, the way they walk, the way they look.

All of your buildings are machines for voyeurism, ever since you designed the restaurant Brasserie in the Seagram Building as a digital hall of mirrors with cameras and monitors.
There was a time when people were really concerned about surveillance. They complained that you couldn't walk around with some camera looking at you, that your privacy was being violated. But now there is a real shift. We're at a point where people are saying, "Oh, nobody's watching me, nobody's looking at me! What's wrong?" Thanks to Facebook and all these other things, we're used to living in public. Of course, it's very strong on the High Line with its succession of views. New Yorkers go there just to watch.

The High Line is also a good example of something you call "post-natural nature". Of course, in Manhattan there was always an element of that. Rem Koolhaas famously wrote about it in his book *Delirious New York*. But I think people are still shocked about all the sharp edges on the High Line. It is the opposite of an oasis.
One of the beautiful things about the High Line is that it wasn't really a place for plants but for machines. When you went up there before we turned it into a park, you realized that this is the stuff of science fiction. The jungle comes back in. Civilization is erased. We always wanted to have that edge between civilization and nature. You feel that the plants could just keep growing up those fingers and move up those cracks and take over.

But at the same time, it's also a world where the machines could take over.
I don't want to disappoint you, but the machines have already taken over. Computers are supposed to help us, instead they tell us what to do: "No, I won't do anything unless you do it the way I do it."

Isn't it time to fight back, then?
Years ago, I read *Last and First Men*, a science fiction novel from 1930 by Olaf Stapledon. It follows the human race to extinction from some new germ developing to some new species developing. It goes on for some 50 billion years. You realize that our time on this planet, although it lasts thousands and thousands of years, is like a flash. We're like mayflies. We'll be gone, we'll be something else. And I personally would rather make that transformation than cling to the ways we've been doing things forever and not moving forward. I'm not a romanticist.

Let's talk about the more immediate future and the ever-increasing importance of the city.
Maybe it's better to think about space first. In the beginning the world was flat, and heaven was above and hell below and everything was really centralized. If you went too far, you fell off the edge of the Earth. Then came the Industrial Revolution with its transportation of goods and people, and suddenly space became distance. Things were measured in terms of distance: prisoners had too little space and a mansion had a great

deal of space. Now space is becoming a quantity of time. We don't say something is five miles away, we say it's ten minutes away or it's eight hours away. Together with what the Internet is doing to our perception, this is a profound change in the way we see space.

Until recently, the car was the dominant factor in the development of cities. What will happen to private mobility?
I don't think the car will disappear. There will always be times when people don't want to be in a bus or an airplane. They want to have the freedom of being an individual and going where they want to go without more than a family around them. Our relationship with the environment will determine whether this car will run on gas, whether it will be electric or a bicycle. I think the bicycle will turn out to be the most efficient way to move from point A to point B in a city. Especially as cities will become denser, people will tend to live more and more within a particular locale, in neighborhoods, and will only occasionally travel to other parts of their city. But I've been around long enough to know that the future is never what you expect it to be. Who knows what the repercussions will be of climate change, the financial crisis, even the oil spill now in the Gulf! I'm trying very desperately to live in the present.

Can you talk about your proposal for the *Audi Urban Future Award*?
There are many people who have retired but who don't want to go to a retirement home, who don't want to live in Florida, who want to enjoy life and see the country. What's happening is they produce instant cities, the world we call RV or caravan. They know there is an event in a particular place. And that small town of 300 people suddenly becomes 3000 people. It is already happening at the Burning Man event, for example. So what kind of infrastructure is needed to make that happen? Should that always be an ad hoc situation? Or could somebody install a point to tie up the vehicles every time they go there? Is there another form of organization? The question is: how can we think of architecture not as a fixed environment but as something that can move from place to place? This could be a model for younger people, too. Let's say I have a job in New York and the company sends me to San Francisco. Or I want to work in Chicago for a while. I just take my residence with me.

This utopia of mobility was very popular in the Nineties. But 9/11, climate change, the rising oil prices and the decline of the middle class have cast quite a pall over it. Is it really still a viable concept?

CITIES WILL BECOME DENSER, PEOPLE WILL TEND TO LIVE MORE AND MORE WITHIN A PARTICULAR LOCALE, IN NEIGHBORHOODS, AND WILL ONLY OCCASIONALLY TRAVEL TO OTHER PARTS OF THEIR CITY.

Yes, absolutely. The world, which was very fragmented, will be much easier to navigate. Barriers are breaking down. Border crossings are much easier. You see this particularly in Europe. China opens up, and the Middle East finally settles down. It's going to be incredible. So when you retire at an age of 65, maybe 70, what do you do? You start traveling. I think that ability to travel, to move around, to find whatever you want, to not be tied to a particular place is going to become very viable again. So either you rent a hotel for a couple of weeks, or your apartment can be sucked out of a steel frame, dropped on a truck base, driven to a port like a container, put on a ship and off you are to Europe. And you can travel around Europe for a couple of months. Why not?

Jörg Häntzschel, born in 1968, studied literature in Berlin, Rennes and London. From 1998 on he wrote for the *Süddeutsche Zeitung*, the *Neue Zürcher Zeitung* and *Die ZEIT*, based first in London and later in New York and focusing primarily on art and architecture. His pieces have appeared in *Architectural Digest*, *Geo* and *Baumeister*. He was head of the features section of the *Süddeutsche Zeitung* (SZ) from 2005 to 2006, and since 2007 he has been the cultural correspondent for the *SZ* in New York.

PRESENTATION DILLER SCOFIDIO + RENFRO

DILLER SCOFIDIO + RENFRO, © AUDI

STATEMENT DILLER SCOFIDIO + RENFRO

NEW YORK, 20 JULY 2010, DILLER SCOFIDIO + RENFRO REGRET TO ANNOUNCE THAT DUE TO SCHEDULING COMPLICATIONS THEY ARE UNABLE TO CONTINUE PARTICIPATION IN THE *AUDI URBAN FUTURE AWARD*, AN INTERNATIONAL ARCHITECTURAL COMPETITION SPONSORED BY AUDI AND CURATED BY STYLEPARK. THE COMPETITION CHALLENGES SIX ARCHITECTURAL TEAMS TO DEVELOP PROPOSITIONS FOR THE FUTURE OF CITIES WITH SPECIFIC EMPHASIS ON INDIVIDUAL AND COLLECTIVE MOBILITY.

"WE ARE HONORED TO HAVE HAD THE CHANCE TO WORK WITH AUDI, AND GREATLY RESPECT THE PREMISE OF THE COMPETITION, WHICH OPENS A DIALOGUE BETWEEN ARCHITECTS AND A MAJOR TRANSPORT MANUFACTURER AS A WAY OF IMAGING BETTER CITIES", COMMENTS DS+R PRINCIPAL CHARLES RENFRO.

DURING ITS THREE-MONTH INVOLVEMENT WITH THE COMPETITION, DILLER SCOFIDIO + RENFRO INVESTIGATED NOTIONS OF THE ITINERANT CITY AND THE FUTURE OF THE RECREATIONAL VEHICLE.

jürgen mayer h.

J. MAYER H. ARCHITECTS
PHOTOS: SABINE REITMAIER, © AUDI

a.way

Once upon a time, around 1985, the world discovered the ozone hole and it changed the way we think about our future. From now on, consumption, production and mobility are at stake. With the introduction of digital technologies in the early 21st century and with electricity as the main source for energy supply, our cities will grow free of pollution and congestion; green, clean, quiet and efficient.

Visions of the future have always been a place of speculation about mobility. The 20th century proposed playful and even sometimes naive visions of flying cars and underwater urban settings. Novel ways of flying around galaxies, journeying to the centre of the earth, diving into submarine worlds, traveling through time, jumping through universes, tele-transporting, injecting into and voyaging through the blood stream of a human body populated our visions of the future. Maybe, in the long term, we will experience these magical modes of transportation. Yet the short-term future might be invisible first.

Individual mobility of the future will strongly be linked to the developments of digitally augmented urban spaces, automated driving and personalized data exchange between the human body and its environment. Traffic will be a constant flow, with no more need for parked vehicles. Pedestrian areas will regain their lost space from cars. Repercussions will be seen on a social, economic and ecological level. Surveillance technologies will transform the city and its inhabitants into a flow of data, blurring the boundaries between body, car and architecture.

New forms of perception will arise from digital technologies. They will allow for each one of us to selectively allow or reject individual aspects of the city. The car will transform from being a viewing machine for maneuvering in traffic towards a sensorial experience machine. Driving through the city will put our senses and sensibilities into the foreground and allow us to interact with the urban context in completely new ways.

And there is always the option of a collapse of all systems that might come as a surprise, keep us going, force us to improvise, invent and move ahead. If at that point cities have proved once more to be flexible, adjustable, able to transform and survive, then we will live under a protecting ozone layer again, happily ever after.

Jürgen Mayer H.

www.jmayerh.com

digital urban cleansing

jürgen mayer h. interviewed by thomas wagner in berlin

In the city of the future, Jürgen Mayer H. is convinced, mobility will be characterized by automated or assisted systems. This will have tremendous repercussions on the infrastructure of inner cities: the automobile will become a "Blickmaschine", a viewing machine for maneuvering in traffic. Traffic lights and street signs will be superfluous; parking garages will be as obsolete as crumple zones and headlights. These changes will create new space for an inward expansion of the city.

In your architecture and urban projects, you often address existing patterns and their superimpositions, drawing conceptual and formal conclusions from their analysis. How would you describe the formative patterns of mobility today and in the future?
The data protection patterns we work with are primarily graphics. What you're talking about are patterns in the sense of general, recurring characteristics. These are two different concepts. Data protection patterns accompany the exchange of information, ensuring that personal information remains encoded until it reaches the intended recipient. Until then, it remains neutral and inaccessible. As such, these patterns do have something to do with transportation. In architectural terms, they represent a specific kind of surface that mediates between content and its appearance or presence much the way a facade mediates between inside and outside, both covering and exposing something; in other words, creating a permeable border between private and public. But where mobility in the city is concerned – and mobility is transportation – we're dealing with a pattern of movement of a very different nature.

What might that pattern of movement look like?
We begin with the assumption that there will no longer be stationary traffic in the city, or rather that the city of the future will no longer allow stationary traffic. What we will have is a constant flow of movement or potential movement that is dynamically present, even though it may prove to be more or less dense at certain times because it adapts to the current mobility requirements or the various intensities of a city during a particular time of year, month, week, or at certain times of the day. In that respect, the pattern that characterizes the city of the future is more of a rhythm: the rhythm of an individual city, something like its pulse. Therefore, the city will need to be constantly monitored; movement within it will have to be continually observed in order to determine when and where there is a need for mobility. New electronic media and forms of communication will play a central role in this; they provide the sensors and the data in order to develop a "city in flux".

Is the continual flow of movement alone decisive? The famous Spanish cellist Pablo Casals once said that "rhythm is all in the delay". Isn't mobility within the city also defined by the alternation between standstill and movement?
In a first step, we're only looking at mobility, in other words, the traffic within a field of buildings. The potential that unfolds with the introduction of automated driving – and we didn't invent that, it's already being developed – is based on increased efficiency. With the help of such systems, i.e. the incorporation of sensors and assistants that take over certain functions, cars can move in closer succession and coordinate their reactions. That fundamentally changes the automobile. A driving machine becomes a viewing machine. That means that the occupant can experience the urban environment in a completely different way, no matter if the car is moving or has to stop or brake.

How will the car change?
Today, the car as a driving machine is only to a limited extent a viewing machine. The windshield limits the horizon, the rear view mirror provides a view behind, headlights are necessary in order to maneuver and navigate in the dark and so on. If the car is transformed into a viewing machine in a broader sense, these parameters lose their significance. If an automobile actually drives itself, many of the

J. MAYER H. ARCHITECTS
PHOTOS: SABINE REITMAIER, © AUDI

things a driver needs today in order to master the task of driving can be eliminated. Not only in the car, but also in the city: As soon as cars are "told" when they need to stop, traffic lights become superfluous. We'll no longer need signs to tell us where we're allowed to turn, because the car will already "know" all of that. And another thing: this kind of car won't need bumpers or a crumple zone, because accidents will be eliminated. That means that when the car changes our behavior will change and the city in which we move will change with it.

What will that mean for individual zones within the city?

There will be zones with varying degrees of automation, from maximum control to no control. The closer one gets to the inner city – today our cities are so full that traffic practically comes to a standstill – the higher the degree of automation. Today I'm only allowed to drive in the inner city if I have a green emissions sticker, because that zone only functions under certain parameters. In the future I'll only be allowed to drive in the inner city if my car is completely automated or has assisted driving capabilities. The important thing is that parameters like a "shared street" can only really work on the basis of such systems. The distinction between street and sidewalk will become obsolete, because each assisted road user maneuvering through the city will be one of many – pedestrians would be similarly equipped.

So you are primarily investigating the effect of an electronically assisted mobility in and on the infrastructure of the inner city. What consequences might that have for buildings?

For example, garages would be superfluous, because automobiles would always be in motion.

Do you mean I'll even be in the car at night?

No, you'll be at home. We'll no longer own cars; we'll use them as needed.

So part of the scenario is a behavioral change along the lines of "using not owning"?

Absolutely. There will not only be less individual ownership, but also less unused capital standing around on the streets. This, by the way, will also improve the mobility systems' innovative capability and increase the speed of innovation. Above all, new spaces will open up within cities. What we are advocating is cleansing the city of all of the tools that are important today in order to make individual mobility within the city possible. Presumably there will be exceptions depending on individual financial means, exclusive options that represent a new kind of luxury. But part of the standard infrastructure will be an option where you pay as necessary and according to distance. Cars will be there if you need one. That will have substantial effects on the city as a whole. We could do without streetlights for the most part because cars would know where they could drive; there will be less noise, fewer emissions, no light pollution, no honking – and a lot more green areas.

Are pedestrians also integrated into the electronic control system?

Yes, but due to their slower speed, they would be less "equipped" and subject to

J. MAYER H. ARCHITECTS
PHOTOS: SABINE REITMAIER, © AUDI

the pattern that characterizes the city of the future is more of a rhythm: the rhythm of an individual city, something like its pulse. therefore, the city will need to be constantly monitored; movement within it will have to be continually observed in order to determine when and where there is a need for mobility.

less control in their movement. The higher the speed of a road user, the more efficient the control and the greater the need to be considerate of more vulnerable road users. There will be more freedom for everyone.

If the possibilities for operating an automobile oneself are reduced, does the car become in some ways more like a means of public transportation? Can we think of such a system in terms of a bus that navigates according to individual demand?
More like a taxi, I would say.

What about the speed of the system? How will you solve the problem of the need for higher transportation capacity at peak hours?
Subway and regional trains will be largely unchanged, whereby we are actually considering how the intervals between trains could be used. How could these systems become more efficient within an interval of three to twenty minutes? I think there's potential there, as well. One thing is certain: Although we are focusing first on individual traffic, there will still be many different mobility systems that exist parallel to one another. But only on the basis of automated driving will the city itself become a mobile system.

Your work can be described as an "architecture of the 'in between'". On the one hand, your buildings often have a sort of sandwich structure, within which there are connections and openings where exchange and communication take place. On the other hand, they pick up on historic and social codes and reprogram them. But there is always an area of 'in between', which also applies to your scenarios for the *Audi Urban Future Award*. In concrete terms, you're not only looking at individual mobility systems, but also at the gaps as uncultivated areas in space or in time. Do you see mobility as taking place within that interval?
One might add that it's also about what is in between the city as we know it today, with its overcrowded spaces, and the city as it will be tomorrow. One often wonders how today's cities manage to function with regards to mobility, because for the most part, these cities already existed before there were automobiles. That also is a sort of gap or 'in between'. We see all of these kinds of 'between' as spaces of possibility. The same thing goes for the buildings we design. If we're successful, they offer possibilities for the perception and use of the building that go beyond the normal function.

So a city saves and stores different eras?
Every historical layer and every development of the city brings forth its own formation, complete with the respective infrastructure. It develops its own mobility formation. If I go to Prague or Seville today, I can see that these cities have more or less successfully adapted to automobile traffic.

We Europeans always talk about the "city center" and take for granted that every city has a center. Is your concept based on the model of a European city or will other models need to be developed for other areas of the world?
Of course, in America, I drive to the shopping mall and cities have a structure that is primarily oriented to the automobile. But there is a need to reduce stationary traffic there, too. That's why we always speak of different city models, of a European city with a center and of a decentralized city. Cities are always condensed areas, however, and that's the important thing when we're talking about urban mobility.

How realistic is such a vision in terms of the capacity of an automated system?
We assume there will have to be a short or long-term buffer to control capacity. There will always be overcapacity at a certain point.

PRESENTATION J. MAYER H. ARCHITECTS
J. MAYER H. ARCHITECTS, © AUDI

BUILDING
STREET
STREET

RED
heel

J. MAYER H. ARCHITECTS
PHOTOS: SABINE REITMAIER, © AUDI

we begin with the assumption that there will no longer be stationary traffic in the city, or rather that the city of the future will no longer allow stationary traffic. what we will have is a constant flow of movement or potential movement that is dynamically present.

MODEL
J. MAYER H. ARCHITECTS, © AUDI

Your scenario comes fairly close to the proposals of the automobile industry: optimization where emissions are concerned, control and networking of various systems. Will that be enough?
We're investigating not only mobility systems but also the effects that changes to those systems will have on the structure and atmosphere of the city. Which of a city's potentials will be given back to the inhabitants? Physical interaction plays a central role in this. For example, how will our relationship to the environment change if our bodies are complemented by digital systems? What we're interested in are the urban rooms for possibility that open up with that kind of technical development. In the 1950's, you drove off in a car to discover the world. Today, we hardly make the distinction between here and away anymore, and there are other possibilities – the Internet is only one – for discovering the world.

But isn't a mental form of travel by necessity deficient, because it's limited to optical and acoustic signals?
For the moment.

How will the social order change in the light of a mixture of media and means of transportation?
The car as we know it today is based on a specific political concept of family. It's designed to accommodate four to five people, the ideal small family. If that changes, the car will have to change too. But individual mobility has to remain affordable.

My question was aiming in the opposite direction: will a change of mobility have an effect on the social order?
If traffic is in constant circulation, emissions-free, stress-free and silent, it will have an effect on the atmosphere in the inner city. Traffic zones will no longer be seen in a negative light, but will be more associated with the idea of living on the waterfront, be it a river, a lake or the ocean. The traffic flows and ripples along. This creates a new atmosphere that will change the way we live together and communicate. Above all the implementation of new technologies and new media will change the interaction between private and public. The additional street space that is gained through the compression of automated cars onto fewer lanes will allow for the creation of a soft zone, an area "in between" buildings and street space, a new room for possibility that would allow for growth and transformation in the middle of the city, where the borders between private and public are constantly renegotiated.

Could your concept be understood – polemically speaking – as an extension of the video arcade by digital means?
It's more than that. If the surface area of streets is reduced, the adjacent buildings can be expanded and a new kind of densification can take place. That means that more people can live in cities and won't need to commute. This would reduce pressure in several ways. What we are trying to accomplish is growth within the city, not of the city itself: an inward expansion.

The city is fragmented differently than it used to be; other patterns and other dissonances are being established. Does that also have an aesthetic effect? Will buildings change due to the fact that they are perceived differently from an automated car?
The introduction of digital assisted systems will change many things, but one thing in particular: everyone will drive through the city with his or her own individual perspective and will perceive those things that are of interest to him or her. Beautiful buildings, people, store windows… in networked systems, the environment will be much more attuned to me and my specific interests. Perhaps it will no longer be necessary for a facade to indicate what type of business or institution is behind it. That information would be communicated to me – selectively. That, too, represents a fragmentation of the city.

So will I be completely lost once I get out of the car or turn off my smart phone?
That kind of system will be a part of us.

Will the city mutate into a self-regulating provisional solution?
I'm not sure if we can go so far as to consider completely new urban structures. The fact is, the systems we are talking about can be adapted to any urban form. They would work just as well in an 18th-century grid plan city as in an uncontrollably growing megacity. What will change are the urban furnishings that support the automobile. Maybe in a few decades, people will bemusedly ask what those colorful signs all over the city were for or what the function of the green and red lights at intersections was.

Will the cleansing of the city be planned just like the car-friendly city once was? Or is the planning optimism of the modern age over?
In a historical context, elements of urban infrastructure have always been kept but were assigned new functions. In the same way that a protective city wall became a ring road, the street will now become something else. In that respect, it's about restructuring usages in an existing territory and an "upgrade" of urban structures.

So in other words, does your concept imply a revision of what is already there? If we take a close enough look and draw the right conclusions, can we see the future taking shape?
The same way that the technological advancement of the railroad in the 19th century brought about an urban expansion with the construction of train stations, we are now about to experience an inward expansion. There's no longer a need for a tabula rasa. The innovation of the city will take place in the form of cybernetic self-innovation.

Thomas Wagner is a member of the Stylepark editorial team and is a contributor to the conception of the *Audi Urban Future Award*. From 1991 to 2007, he was editor for art and design at the *Frankfurter Allgemeine Zeitung*, and today he works as a freelance writer and art critic. He is an honorary professor at the Academy of Fine Arts in Nuremberg and recently published the volume *Licht im Schacht von Babel*, including texts on the documenta in Kassel and the Art Biennale in Venice.

a driving machine becomes a viewing machine. that means that the occupant can experience the urban environment in a completely different way, no matter if the car is moving or has to stop or brake. what we are advocating is cleansing the city of all of the tools that are important today in order to make individual mobility within the city possible.

J. MAYER H. ARCHITECTS
PHOTOS: SABINE REITMAIER, © AUDI

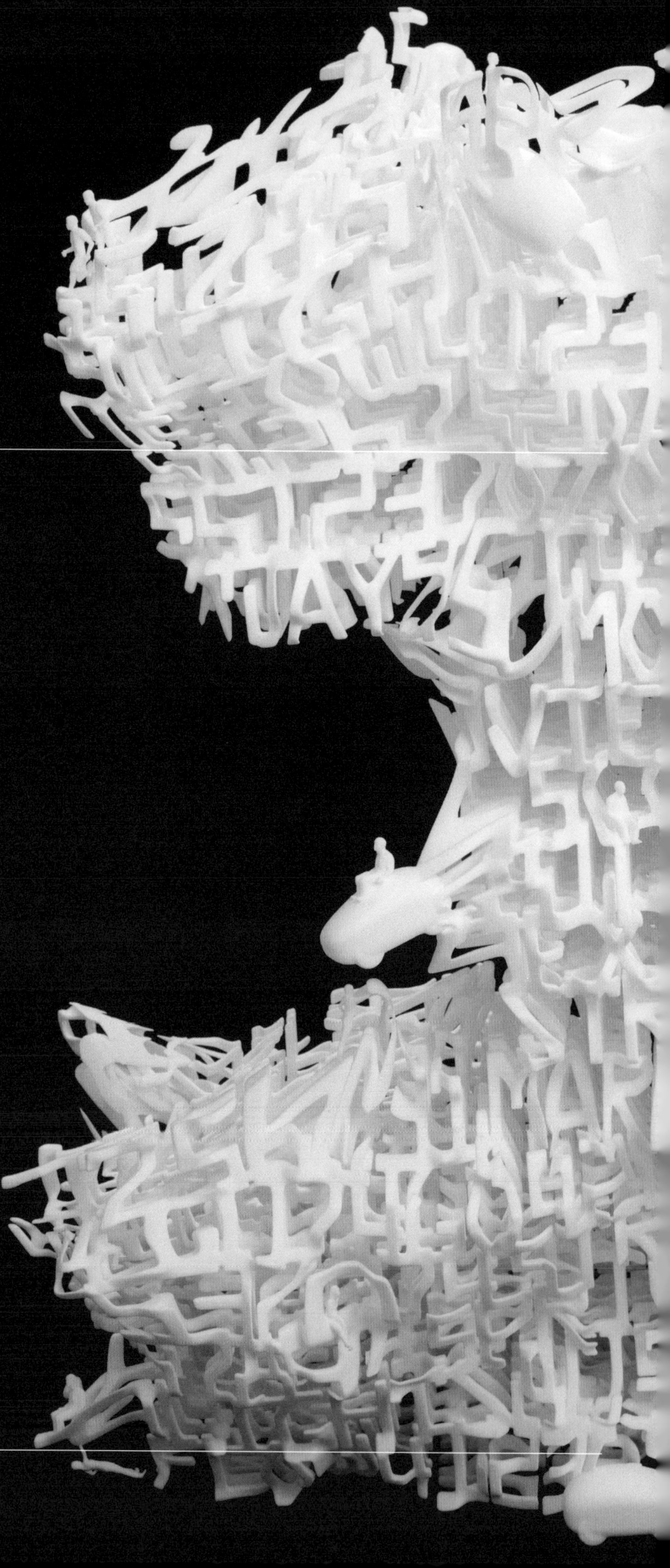

MODEL
J. MAYER H. ARCHITECTS, © AUDI

STANDARD-ARCHITECTURE

STANDARDARCHITECTURE
PHOTOS: ERIC GREGORY POWELL, © AUDI

HARMONIOUS BEIJING

Beijing has re-invented itself in the past 20 years, changing from what was once a historic city into a futuristic city. The city has expanded outwards through one new ring road after another. This "road first" approach to planning and the resulting uncontrolled outward sprawl have become a typical model of Chinese urbanization.

SUBWAY RING CITY

Why do we still plan our new cities with the age-old "road-first" infrastructure? There are five million cars in Beijing now. In five years there will be far more cars in Beijing than the total area of roads can support: there will be zero mobility on the roads inside the city.

There is no doubt that Beijing will continue to expand with Chinese speed and on a Chinese scale during the next 20 years. But in the coming decades, the increasing pressure of urban pollution and shortages of fossil fuels, farmland and road space will make it necessary to re-define the model for expansion.

Harmonious Beijing is seeking a new vision of urbanization and urban mobility for Beijing in 2030. It will adopt a "subway first" development model to replace the "road first" growth model, and new urban developments will take place only along the new series of subway rings of this powerful transportation system.

3D CITY PLANNING

The Beijing planning bureau will adopt and implement 3D imaging in infrastructure planning, so that land definition will no longer be represented in 2D by red line boundaries on paper. This will allow for a series of government-developed, 1500-meter-high "meta-mountains" that are directly connected to the subway rings to be visualized as three-dimensional volumes in a digital 3D model.

LINEAR CITY CENTER

This infrastructure, a ring of inter-connected subway lines and meta-mountains around the city, will form a "linear city center" that can accommodate all kinds of urban programs with a highly efficient and convenient public transportation system.

STANDARDARCHITECTURE
PHOTOS: ERIC GREGORY POWELL, © AUDI

TRAVEL BELTS

Inside the city, the current roads will be upgraded into "travel belts", electrically driven belts that move vehicles and people around the city at a speed of 60–80 kilometers per hour. People are not allowed to drive their cars while on the belts, thus dramatically reducing carbon emissions and at the same time changing the lifestyle of the time spent on the road.

TRAVEL BELT BUBBLES

The Travel Belt Bubble is a type of auto-drive electric vehicle that will travel with the "travel belts" as well as move between them. The space inside the vehicle is personally adaptable and can be used as a living, working, sleeping, or entertainment space while traveling on the belts. People can also go out and socialize with other bubblers within the moving public realm, or the bubbles can be attached together to form a semi-public group vehicle. Travel Belt Bubbles will be more than just cars; they can be designed and utilized as mobile houses and mobile offices.

AGRI-URBANIZATION

Agriculture will be re-introduced into the urban area of Beijing. Rooftops will be transformed into farmland to produce food for local consumption, and the outer surfaces of all buildings will be sprayed with a new type of bio-paint that will create a kind of moss-growing surface, thus maximizing oxygen production in the city.

standardarchitecture

www.standardarchitecture.cn

HARMONIOUS BEIJING

STANDARDARCHITECTURE, © AUDI

A RING OF MOVING ROADS

STANDARDARCHITECTURE, © AUDI

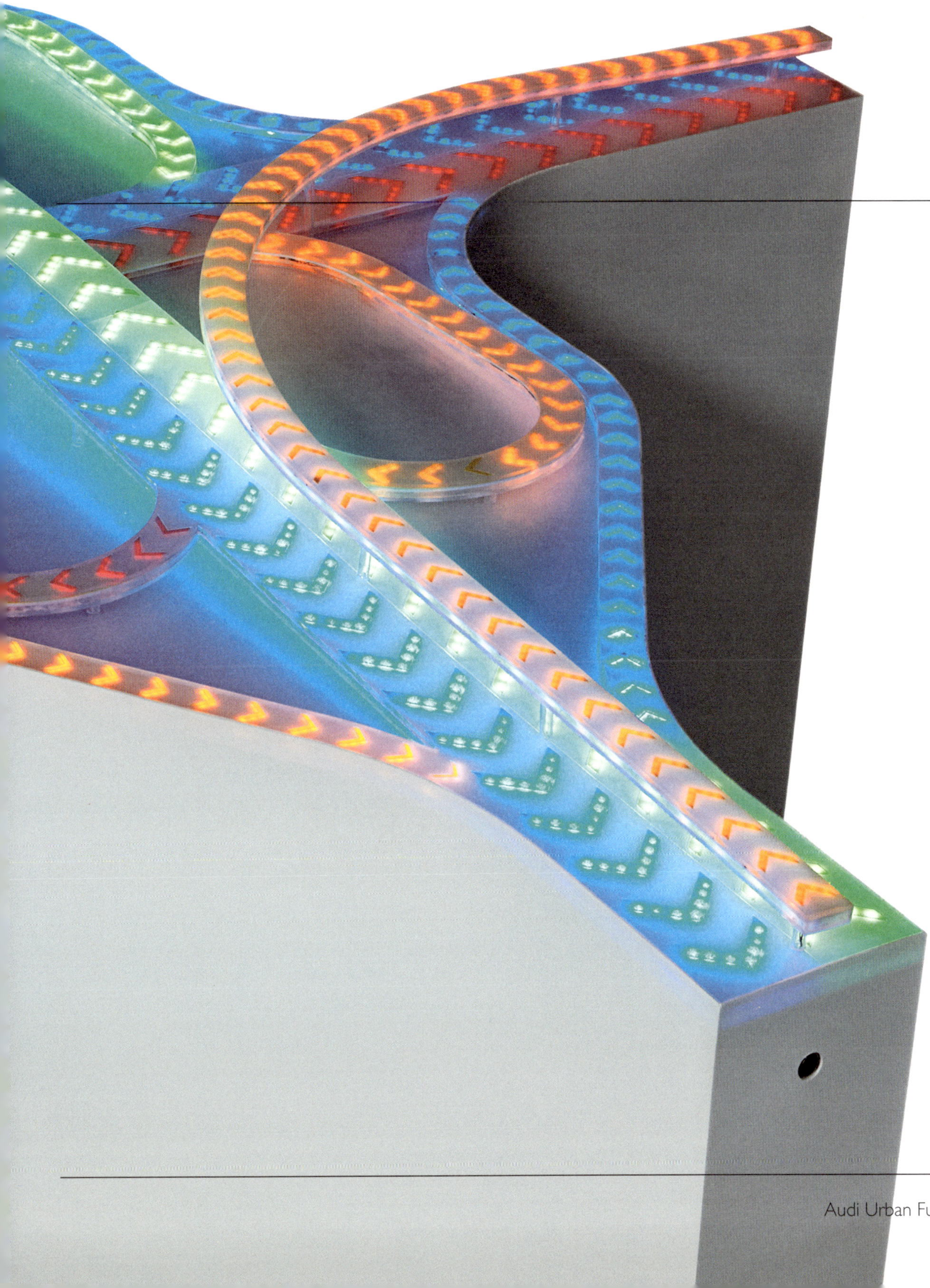

REVOLUTION IN THE THIRD DIMENSION

ZHANG KE INTERVIEWED BY ARIC CHEN IN BEIJING

Based in Beijing, Standardarchitecture is at the forefront of a generation of young, cutting-edge design firms who are transforming architecture in China. Founded in 2001 by Zhang Ke, a graduate of Beijing's Tsinghua University and Harvard's Graduate School of Design, the award-winning studio now includes four partners who share its global perspective nuanced by a localized approach. Also called by its abbreviation, ST.AR.T, the firm's projects span from the highly acclaimed Yaluntzangpu Boat Terminal in Tibet and the Qingcheng Mountain Teahouse in Chengdu to the proposed 160-meter-tall Dancing Book Towers in Wuchang, alongside experimental urban planning visions for Hong Kong and Xi'an. Aric Chen spoke with Zhang Ke on the future transformation of the urban center and on his vision for a "harmonious Beijing".

You recently abbreviated the name of your firm, from Standardarchitecture to ST.AR.T. How come?
From the beginning, we chose Standardarchitecture because it's very neutral, it doesn't imply any specific form and it goes back to the fundamentals. For example, we focus a lot on local materials and urban spaces. And we're not bound by what's already established, which is why we like the name ST.AR.T, or "STandardARchitecture Team." For every project, we want a completely new "start" in terms of throwing off all preconceptions, especially formal preconceptions. We're almost pretending we don't know anything, so we can find different ways and new possibilities for doing things. It's a process of daydreaming but at the same time of being pragmatic and seeing how we can bring these seemingly impossible things into reality.

So what was your "starting" point for thinking about the future of the city?
There are at least two layers to consider. The first relates to how we urbanize. In Beijing, for example, in the '60s, we had the Second Ring Road, and then in the '80s we built the Third Ring, in the '90s the Fourth Ring, around 2000 the Fifth, and now we have the Sixth and Seventh. So the biggest problem we have in China is that our cities are expanding and sprawling outward without end. It's putting even bigger pressure on the center while taking up precious agricultural land. And, of course, it's worsening pollution. There are millions of cars stuck in traffic, not moving at all, on the Ring Roads, and it's only getting worse. Last year, 1.3 million cars were sold just in Beijing; this year it's expected to be two million. So there's a need to rethink or redefine our patterns of urbanization, which can change our future cities very dramatically for the better.

In our proposal, we shift planning from a "road first" to a "subway first" model. We provide the city with a boundary to contain the sprawl, and a powerful public transportation system underneath. It's not one single line but a parallel, powerful infrastructure of subways with very tall buildings or multipurpose structures built on top. So you can go from each tower directly into the subway and on from there. This new infrastructure will still provide a lot of room for growth that is not outward expansion, but rather an upward and inward expansion. At the same time it changes the form of the central business district from a center-point one to a linear one. And then we reclaim space for agriculture – we call it Agricurbanism – and use it as a means of urbanization. We bring it back into the center of the city, to the tops and outer surfaces of buildings. Also, we think technology will help advance new ways of planning. Land definition will no longer be a sheet of paper with lines – that seems ancient now – but rather a 3D model. We call it 3D planning. And so the government isn't just going to develop infrastructure with roads. It's going to develop these tall – 1,500-meter tall – structures that are not finished, but with all the horizontal and vertical infrastructure built in. If you're a developer, instead of buying a 2D piece of land, you'll buy a 3D volume of land.

There are a lot of complex mechanisms at work, including policy, government and economics. But what about cultural factors?

PHOTOS: ERIC GREGORY POWELL, © AUDI

That's the second layer. We should never forget that it's people who live in cities, so it's fascinating to explore the possible lifestyle changes of people moving around in a cleaner, happier way.

Is this where mobility and the automobile come in?
We came up with what we call Travel Belts. At the beginning, we made the statement that in the future there will be no individual cars within the city. But that was a bit too utopian and unrealistic. So then we thought of a hybrid way. Everyone's been talking about cars moving on roads, but what if the roads – in Beijing, the Ring Roads – moved and the cars stood still? As Travel Belts, these roads would be safer for passengers, while becoming great public spaces. You can get out of your car, chat with the person in the next car, fly a kite and hang out. You could have shopping cars and mobile office cars. You may think this is impossible, but it's absolutely not. It's like in the late 1930s, when GM proposed the first highway and everyone thought it was insanely impossible. And then, less than 50 years later, highways are everywhere in the world. Our roads have to be upgraded to a more high-tech status that can actually save energy and make our lives more convenient, while improving communication and social interaction. It's about making the roads more advanced, not just the cars. Of course, there will be a difference between what we'll need within cities and between them. But I think individual cars can stay pretty much similar to what's being developed now: hybrid cars, electric cars and hydrogen cars, with more bullet trains for intercity mobility.

But explain your concept of the Travel Belt Bubble.
It's an example of something we designed for these hybrid Travel Belts and, of course, it doesn't exclude other forms of vehicles at all. We are thinking of mobility in terms of both collective and individual mobility. We have always divided them, saying, OK, this is public transportation and these are private, individual cars. However, I think there might be some space in between, a form of individual mobility that works together with an upgraded public road system. So the Travel Belt Bubbles are individual vehicles, with the seats back-to-back to maximize space in a very simple form. Computers do the work, so you can fold down the seats and use them as a mobile office. There are lots of possibilities you can start to think of. You can also link them together, so the bus driver is no longer guiding one big bus, but rather the head Bubble or the head Baby, with all the other Babies trailing behind. It's like kindergarten; you're the teacher holding the rope. But I don't think it will be the vehicles that will change the infrastructure; it's going to be the other way around.

What role does luxury play in this kind of pseudo-private vehicle scenario?
The luxury, or premium, thing is still going to be there. You'll also still need electric charging or battery charging stations. What we are thinking about is: which technologies are available now and in the very near future, and by applying them, what are the possibilities for upgrading the whole urban infrastructure so that we can solve the problems on a massive scale?

In this context, how do the private sector and companies like Audi fit in?
I think what Audi is doing is very interesting, initiating this project and thinking of the urban future in a way that provides a lot of inspiration. For us, it was a chance to think more broadly and independently in comparison to when you work for a client. You gain a bit of a detached perspective and see a more thorough picture – the more real, pragmatic problems of the city – and then the whole thing becomes more valid. There's some purity. Audi is the initiator and sponsor of this event, and I think companies can definitely offer new ideas and help move things forward. But in the end, it's really up to the policymakers. It's interesting, though, because the ideas can start from the bottom up and then somehow reach the understanding of the top level because, in China, a lot of the policymakers now are younger and very open,

STANDARDARCHITECTURE
PHOTOS: ERIC GREGORY POWELL, © AUDI

MODEL HARMONIOUS BEIJING
PHOTOS: ERIC GREGORY POWELL, © AUDI

WE SHOULD NEVER FORGET THAT IT'S PEOPLE WHO LIVE IN CITIES, SO IT'S FASCINATING TO EXPLORE THE POSSIBLE LIFESTYLE CHANGES OF PEOPLE MOVING AROUND IN A CLEANER, HAPPIER WAY.

IN THE PAST 20 YEARS, WE URBANIZED 200 MILLION FARMERS IN CHINA; IN THE NEXT 20 YEARS WE WILL EITHER SEE ANOTHER 400 MILLION PEOPLE MOVE FROM THE COUNTRYSIDE TO THE CITIES, OR SMALL AND MEDIUM TOWNS WILL BECOME MEDIUM-SIZED CITIES THROUGH THE PROCESS OF ON-THE-SPOT URBANIZATION.

So how close or far away do you think the future is?
I think we have to talk about time frame differences. I grew up in Beijing, in China, and the change that's happened in 20 years here would take maybe 50 or 60 in the West. So our year 2030 could also mean 2060 or 2090 for Europe.

Do you see China and Europe developing on parallel tracks?
Currently, yes. But the pressures are also different. In the past 20 years, we urbanized 200 million farmers in China; in the next 20 years we will either see another 400 million people move from the countryside to the cities, or small and medium towns will become medium-sized cities through the process of on-the-spot urbanization.

Obviously, one can't apply models uniformly across cultures and places. But do you see China as a laboratory from which the rest of the world can learn?
Absolutely. We talk about evolution versus revolution, but I think what's happening here in China may possibly become a kind of urban infrastructure revolution. It started with a very fast, almost accidental happening and became a more consciously planned urban experimentation due to the pressures of climate change, energy shortages and so on. If we experiment at such a speed and scale, there are going to be some good lessons or experiences that other parts of the world can learn from.

Is this yet another example of China leapfrogging?
You mean the new Great Leapfrog Forward? Actually, I don't think it's leapfrogging. Everything is moving at such a fast speed that it looks like leapfrogging. But it's just very fast progress.

Aric Chen is an independent writer, critic and curator based in Beijing and New York. He currently contributes to publications including the *New York Times*, *Wallpaper*, *Architectural Record* and *Surface*, and has organized exhibitions and projects at venues spanning from Art Basel Miami Beach/Design Miami, ExperimentaDesign Amsterdam and the Saint-Etienne International Design Biennale to New York's Center for Architecture and the Design Museum Holon. In 2008 and 2009 he served as founding co-creative director of 100% Design Shanghai, affiliated with the 100% Design fairs in London and Tokyo.

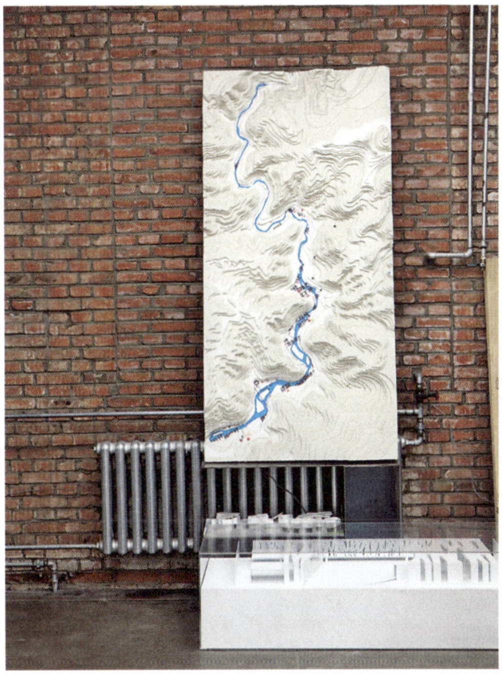

STANDARDARCHITECTURE
PHOTOS: ERIC GREGORY POWELL, © AUDI

SCUOLA GRANDE DI SANTA MARIA DELLA MISERICORDIA
PHOTOS: MICHELE CROSERA, © AUDI

THE UNFINISHED PALACE JACOPO SANSOVINO'S SCUOLA GRANDE DI SANTA MARIA DELLA MISERICORDIA IN VENICE

BY HORANT FASSBINDER

For all its magnificence, the mighty brick box of the Misericordia – or, more precisely, the building's design – doesn't make the impression of representing a great moment in architectural history. Yet anyone entering the great hall on the ground floor will at least be aware that not only this space, but also the entire building is based on a plan of great beauty and the highest sophistication. The author, Jacopo Sansovino, developed a formal language specifically for this project in 1531 that was later, in his buildings on the Piazza San Marco, to become the epitome of the Venetian architecture of his day.

Its patron was one of the five charitable confraternities that in Venice were known as *Scuole Grandi*, due to their substantial membership and wealth. They were joined by their common adoration of a saint or, as in this case, of the Mother of God, with the aim of winning their blessing for their fellow brothers and for the city, in particular through works of charity (*misericordia*) in the name of their respective patron saint. The *Scuole Grandi* administered great fortunes, which they amassed through donations, testaments and membership fees, and they used them to support brothers in need and occasionally other impoverished people. They each counted some five hundred members, about one-tenth of whom were established, wealthy yet not aristocratic and therefore politically powerless Venetians, the so-called *Cittadini*. Only they had voting privileges in the *Scuole Grandi*, only they occupied leading positions in these institutions of eminent importance for the social structure of the city, which served to further the interests of the *Cittadini* without disturbing the existing balance of power.

In the course of the 15th century, the role of the *Scuole Grandi* as a platform for cultivation of the image of the *Cittadini* grew. They continually sought to outdo one another with the most magnificent furnishings in the numerous processions and, particularly after c. 1450, the competition for the most impressive *Scuole* building became increasingly fierce. The 1498 decision of the Misericordia, despite its weak financial state, to give up its old building – which was supposedly dilapidated but is still standing today – and to build in honor of God and the Virgin Mary, as is repeatedly stated in the resolutions, a new *Scuola* that would outshine all others in terms of its size and conspicuous position, can only be understood in this context. The openly expressed will to prevail in the battle of the *Scuole Grandi* rendered the Misericordia blind to its wholly insufficient means to finance the gigantic project, as its unfinished state still impressively testifies even today.

Apart from its intended grandeur and its originally exposed position, the program of the new building made no departure from the usual plan of the *Scuole Grandi*: A grand hall on the ground floor served not only as a foyer, but also accommodated preparations for the intricate processions and the distribution of assistance to the poor. From here, an imposing stairway led to an equally large hall with an altar on the upper floor, where the brotherhood celebrated mass on Sundays and where the *Cittadini* elected the substantial, annually changing leadership of the *Scuola*. A smaller room adjacent to the upper hall, the albergo, was used for official duties. The exterior of the *Scuole Grandi* reflected their double religious and secular role: The "church" of a Christian brotherhood with a symmetrical, gabled tripartite facade and religious artistic embellishment, but at the same time a "palace", the location of collective, secular decisions of the *Cittadini* with a great, many-windowed main hall on the *piano nobile*, much like the Palazzo Ducale of the nobles.

Not long after the decision for the new building was made, a long and, for Venice, disastrous war (1508–29) forced construction to a halt. When, after 1530, one could finally think about recommencing work on the building, the foundations had already been laid and the proportions of the building thus determined, but the original plans were no longer modern. Following a competition among four architects in the year 1531, the *Scuola* decided on the elaborate project of the architect and sculptor Jacopo Sansovino, who had fled to Venice from Rome in 1527, following the city's devastation at the hands of the Landsknechts. He had not yet realized any buildings in Venice, yet was well respected for the success of his restoration work on the domes of San Marco.

Sansovino's design is most effectively assessed from the perspective of the great hall on the ground floor. As in the other *Scuole*, the ceiling is supported by two long rows of columns on high pedestals. However, the spacing between the supports is not uniform, as was the practice up to that time, but rather the columns alternate in a-b-a-b, giving the room a rhythmic quality. In a marked contrast to the other *Scuole Grandi*, the columns are organic, upward-growing bodies. As if effortlessly, their leafy capitals support richly decorated entablature with a stone-like surface treatment that, in turn, carries the roof. The walls respond to the two rows of freestanding columns with half-columns; the entablature becomes a relief. Large windows are arranged in the broad wall panels, with the smaller intervals occupied by reliefs alluding to divine patronage and finely framed sculpture niches, whose hollow form enhances the volume of the wall columns through contrast.

The organization of the facades was planned to correspond with the interior walls. The verticals of the brick exterior were intended to recall the half columns; the horizontally projecting rows of bricks were meant to secure the entablature. On the upper floor, the composition of the lower wall was to be repeated on the inside and outside with slight variation. The brick would have been concealed by white Istrian limestone. The alternation of convex and concave forms, a rich decoration of fine profiles, smaller columns in the window frames, reliefs and sculptures would have served to enliven the architectural framework, upon whose bright surface light would have been reflected from the waves.

Sansovino spoke a language that was as yet unknown in Venice. Its generosity, reference to antiquity, its finely scaled proportions and the consistency with which sculptural decoration became part of the design were qualities as obvious as the crystalline clarity of its consistent connection between the interior and the exterior. The leading heads of the *Scuola* knew that this was the language of Vitruvius, interpreted through the avant-garde of architects like Sansovino who practiced in Rome until 1527 and whose teachings had been distributed internationally in etchings and books.

In 1531, this language was not yet in the least bit Venetian. If the *Scuola* selected Sansovino's design regardless, it was surely only because it easily topped the buildings of the other *Scuole Grandi*. Of similar importance was likely the fact that, in those days, many in Venice felt the time was ripe for a change. The city republic had suffered severe defeat in the long war between 1508 and 1529. In the future, its former self-satisfaction would no longer be possible, *la Serenissima* now had to represent her power and stature to an international audience and in an international language, while concealing her real demise.

Sansovino, who mastered this language like no one else, was soon to be commissioned by the state with the redevelopment for prestige reasons of the city center – above all with the Loggetta and the Biblioteca Marciana (1537/38) opposite the Palazzo Ducale. It was now becoming ever more clear that his forms were those of the nobility that governed the city, and not those of the *Cittadini* with their much more conventional aesthetics. That strengthened the sizable faction of Misericordia brothers who had been against Sansovino's design from the very beginning. Not merely aesthetic reasons, but rather primarily financial concerns moved the *Scuola* to make alterations to the project, which was progressing slowly due to lack of funds, that soon led to its disfiguration.

Not until over fifty years after construction was begun, and nineteen years after Jacopo Sansovino's death, could the confraternity finally move into the unfinished building that had only provisionally been made functional. Aside from a later staircase addition, the *Scuola* today still reflects the state of construction that had then been reached. Neither the vaulted ceiling planned in the upper hall nor its wall composition, neither the *albergo* nor the revolutionary three-flighted staircase, a splendid stage for ascending and descending, were completed. Only the great hall on the ground floor, albeit with greatly reduced and simplified windows, and the brick substructure of the intended limestone facade reflect Sansovino's design.

Nonetheless, what is there suffices for our fantasy to construct the rhythmically composed, richly decorated, white and highly visible building, allowing it to take shape in the language that we know from Sansovino's buildings on the Piazza San Marco. In its transparent clarity, its precise and yet vital and lively order, the design is representative of the High Renaissance ideal of a world created by human deeds and human intellect, harmonious in its order with a high quality of life. In its present condition, the building is as much a testimony to these wonderful ambitions as to their demise.

Horant Fassbinder studied art history, history, philosophy and languages, architecture and urban planning. He has been a professor at the Braunschweig School of Fine Arts in Germany since 1977, with areas of specialization in architectural history and contemporary art.

SCUOLA GRANDE DI SANTA MARIA DELLA MISERICORDIA
PHOTOS: MICHELE CROSERA, © AUDI

SCUOLA GRANDE DI SANTA MARIA DELLA MISERICORDIA
PHOTOS: MICHELE CROSERA, © AUDI

A SKYLINE BUILT OF SPACE AND TIME

RAUMLABORBERLIN'S EXHIBITION ARCHITECTURE

Raumlaborberlin is a collective of eight architects and artists who, in various interdisciplinary project teams, have been developing concepts at the interface between culture and urban planning since 1999. The group's installations, performances, exhibitions and temporary structures focus on public space and its perception; they are to be understood as architectural and artistic interventions. Raumlaborberlin's interdisciplinary approach transcends any given genre, and the collective's own areas of focus are complemented through collaboration with external partners and specialists. In 2008, the Kunstraum in Munich and the Heidelberg Kunstverein dedicated individual exhibitions to the group. Raumlaborberlin has been represented at the perhaps most important architecture exhibition worldwide, the Architecture Biennale in Venice, regularly since 2004. The group garnered international attention with, among others, the Gasthof Bergkristall (2005), a temporary hotel set up in the Palace of the Republic in Berlin prior to its demolition. Current projects include "The Knot", a cooperative platform for art in public spaces in Berlin, Warsaw and Bucharest (2010), and the Raumlabor exhibition entitled Bye Bye Utopia, which opened at the Kunsthaus Bregenz in July. For the *Audi Urban Future Award*, Raumlaborberlin designed the exhibition architecture at the Scuola Grande della Misericordia in Venice.

The city of the future in the context of mobility issues, and possibly even in a utopian sense, is the theme of the *Audi Urban Future Award 2010*. For the exhibition at the Scuola Grande di Santa Maria della Misericordia in Venice, by Venetian standards a relatively large and nearly free-standing historical building, Raumlaborberlin designed a modular, concentrated and object-like exhibition architecture consisting of a succession of linear aisles connected by "tabbed" walls like the dividing pages of an index. Raumlaborberlin treats the exhibition as a public domain itself, following Giambattista Nolli's interpretation: in his "Pianta di Roma" (1748), he incorporated all spaces that were accessible to an urban public into the map, in addition to streets and open squares. Raumlaborberlin also adheres to Mauricio Cobalan's definition of public space as a place that is created wherever people come together and exchange views.

Viewed from the outside, the modular character of the exhibition architecture with its elements of varying heights recalls the silhouette of a city. Like an abstract skyline, the modules form different areas, strive upward, descend like steps or are nested inside one another. Visitors can also climb up to a platform and gain an overhead view of the entire exhibition space in all its facets, as if from a tower. The exhibition architecture is thus not merely narrative, but also invites visitors to participate physically by exploring the structure's interior according to their own plan, immersing themselves in individual spaces and contributions or surveying the entire exhibition terrain. There are also areas that invite one to linger and take a break; rather than demanding physical discipline from visitors, the exhibition offers opportunities to relax and rest, to find a place to process what one has seen, to talk or simply to watch.

Within this structure, each of the five competition contributions has the space of one aisle for its presentation. The aisles are identified by individual color schemes, so that the contributions can be clearly distinguished from one another optically. The colors are derived from the color concept of the competition, so that the presentation in the exhibition can be linked to those in other media. The linear progression of the individual aisles underscores the importance of the process for the competition and represents the path leading to the end result of each contribution.

Within this predetermined structure, competition participants were asked to interpret their designated space in the spirit of their approach and to thus claim their individual area for themselves. In this way, the exhibition architecture provides a framework that is modified in dialogue with the individual participants.

The aisles are not simply straight, but rather follow a complex and convoluted geometry. Niches, projections and recesses contribute structure and allow for the presentation of models, plans, sketches, photographs, films and text. Unexpected openings in the walls between the aisles allow viewers to cross over into neighboring project areas. Intersections and transitional passageways allow for an alternative reading of the exhibition. The cross-passages serve to illustrate the fact that ideas do not merely spring from the mind of a genius but are always rooted in a society and an age, in other words, that good ideas are based upon contemporary inspiration, upon earlier ideas of others, and on a dialogue with other experts. These shortcuts allow visitors to the exhibition to select their own path, to move from one world of ideas to the next, to identify parallels or differences, and to contrast and compare works directly. The exhibition architecture thus fulfills two functions: It provides a guideline and a system of orientation while allowing for the individual selection of combinations, for individual intake and interpretation. This creates an atmosphere of enthusiastic discovery that is, at the same time, a renouncement of didactic presentation models that dictate the behavior of the viewer.

Visitors to the exhibition are not only offered individual insights and outlooks, they may also take in the different areas bit by bit, in the spirit of Henri Lefebvre's fundamental assessment of the urban as "pure form: a place of encounter, assembly, simultaneity."*

Raumlaborberlin

* H. Lefebvre, *The Urban Revolution*, transl. R. Bononno (Minneapolis, 2003) p. 118.

www.raumlabor-berlin.de

CLOUD 9
ALISON BROOKS ARCHITECTS

GROUP
STANDARD-ARCHITECTURE
ALISON BROOKS ARCHITECTS

EXHIBITION ARCHITECTURE FOR THE AUDI URBAN FUTURE AWARD 2010 IN THE SCUOLA GRANDE DI SANTA MARIADELLA MISERICORDIA IN VENICE
RAUMLABORBERLIN, © AUDI

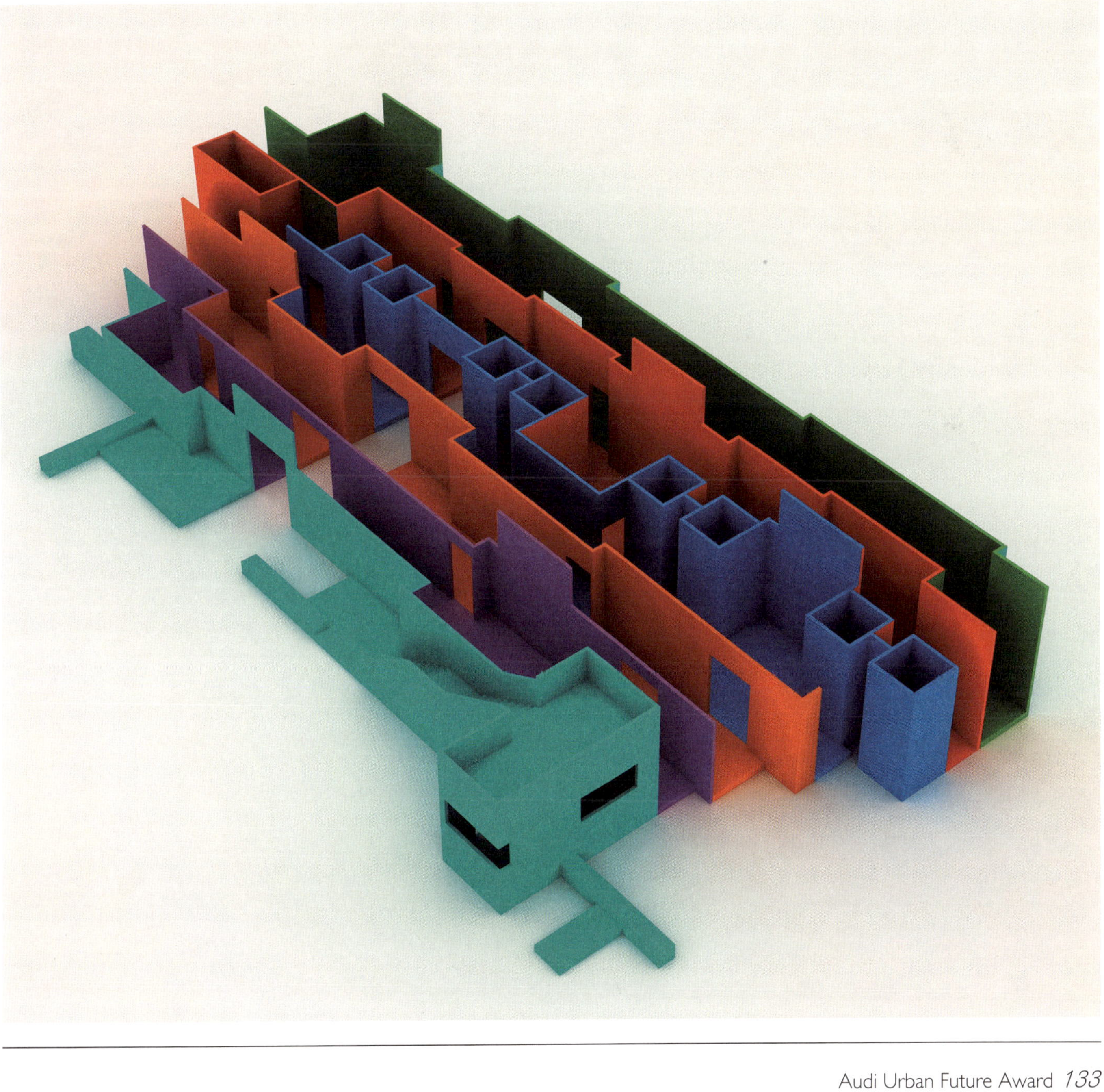

JURY

WOLFGANG EGGER is Head of Audi Group Design. Following his studies of Industrial Design at the College of Arts and Sciences in Milan, Egger began his career in 1989 as an exterior designer for Alfa Romeo, where he became Senior Designer for exteriors at the Centro Stile Alfa Romeo in 1993. He joined Seat in Spain in 1998, where he oversaw the development of the Altea and Leon series production vehicles as well as the studies Concept Salsa, Concept Emotión and Concept Tango. Egger was named Head of Centro Stile Lancia in 2001. During the same year, he transferred to the Centro Stile Alfa Romeo, where he held the same position and led work on the development of the Alfa models 147GTA, 159 and 159 Sportwagon, Brera, Concept 8c Competizione and Concept 8c Spider, among others. Since May 2007, Egger has been Head of Audi Group Design in Ingolstadt and, as such, carries full design responsibility for the Audi and Lamborghini brands.

CHRISTIAN GÄRTNER is Director of Stylepark AG. He studied Economics in Heidelberg and Berlin and worked as a consultant for several years before becoming one of the co-founders of the Internet platform Stylepark in Frankfurt/Main in 2000. Since then, Gärtner has initiated, conceived and contributed to diverse projects in the areas of design and architecture, including *Stylepark in Residence* at the imm cologne and *The Design Annual*, in cooperation with Messe Frankfurt. Moreover, he advises companies on the development and optimization of specific competencies in all areas of design. In the competition for the *Audi Urban Future Award*, Christian Gärtner assumes the dual role of curator and member of the jury.

ANDRES LEPIK is Curator of the Architecture and Design Department at the Museum of Modern Art in New York. Following his studies of Art History and German Literature in Augsburg and Munich, he earned a PhD in Rome with a dissertation entitled *Architectural Models of the Renaissance*. Lepik joined the Neue Nationalgalerie in Berlin as a curator in 1994. From 2004 to 2007, he was Curator for the Architecture of the 20th and 21st Centuries at the Kunstbibliothek, Staatliche Museen zu Berlin. He has been with the Museum of Modern Art since 2007. Among the architectural exhibitions he has curated are *Renzo Piano* (2000), *Content/Rem Koolhaas and AMO/OMA* (2003/2004), *Oswald Mathias Ungers. Cosmos of Architecture* (2006) and *In Situ. Architecture and Landscape* (2009). Lepik is the author of numerous books and articles on the architecture of the 20th and 21st centuries.

JUN MA is Vice Dean of the School of Automotive Studies at Tongji University in Shanghai. After graduating from the Technische Universität Darmstadt with a degree in Automotive Electronics, Jun Ma gained 15 years of experience in the automotive industry, seven in electronic development and six in marketing and after-sales. He was responsible for technical development, marketing and management at both Conti Teves and Audi. In 2004, he followed an invitation from Wan Gang, a former Audi colleague and Minister of Economics and Technology in China since 2007, to teach at the Tongji University in Shanghai. Jun Ma serves as Vice Secretary of the Shanghai FCV Partnership and as an automotive engineering expert for diverse associations and political advisory boards for the Chinese automobile industry.

RAHUL MEHROTRA teaches at the Massachusetts Institute of Technology and heads the architectural firm RMA Architects in Mumbai. Following his studies in Architecture in Ahmedabad, India, he attended the Harvard Graduate School of Design. Mehrotra founded his own practice in 1990, which today goes by the name of RMA Architects. As an architect and urban planner, he has since focused intensively on urban renewal and conservation projects. Several of his designs have received awards, including the Lakshmi Machine Works corporate office in Coimbatore, India. Mehrotra's studies and publications focus on urban development throughout India and in Mumbai in particular. As an activist and consultant, Mehrotra is dedicated to the issue of the conservation of historical buildings in Mumbai. He has been Executive Director of the Urban Design Research Institute in Mumbai since 1994 and, since 2007, Professor at the MIT School of Architecture and Urban Planning.

FERNANDO DE MELLO FRANCO is Professor at São Judas Tadeu University in São Paulo. After graduating from the Faculty of Architecture and Urbanism in São Paulo, de Mello Franco became a Design Critic at the Graduate School of Design at Harvard, where he began collaboration with the landscape architect Christian Werthmann, which resulted in the 2009 study and exhibition entitled *Tactical Operations in the Informal City*. Together with Marta Moreira and Milton Braga, de Mello Franco founded MMBB Architects in São Paulo in 1990. Notable areas of focus within the broad spectrum covered in his projects and investigations are urban mobility systems and water resources management. His research was recognized with the Best Entry Award at the Rotterdam International Biennale in 2007. Among other exhibitions, de Mello Franco co-authored the exhibition *São Paulo: networks and places* at the 2006 Venice Biennale.

SASKIA SASSEN is Professor of Sociology at Columbia University in New York and Chairman of the Jury for the *Audi Urban Future Award*. Born in the Netherlands, Sassen grew up in Argentina and Italy. She studied Sociology, Philosophy and Economics at the University of Notre Dame in Indiana, USA, at the Université de Poitiers in France and at Harvard University. In her international research activities, Sassen addresses themes of globalization in a social, economic and political context as well as questions relating to migration and the development of urban agglomerations and megacities. As a sociologist and economist, she coined the concept of the "global city" in the 1990s. For her five-year UNESCO research project "Sustainable Human Settlement", which was completed in 2005, Sassen established a scholarly network in over 30 countries. She is the Robert S. Lynd Professor for Sociology and a member of the Committee on Global Thought at Columbia University. Her publications, which include *The Global City* (1991, 2nd edition 2001), *Cities in a World Economy* (1994, 3rd edition 2006), and *Territory, Authority, Rights: From Medieval to Global Assemblages* (2006) have been translated into 21 languages.

STEFAN SIELAFF is Head of Audi Design. Following his studies in Industrial Design at the FH Munich, he went on to study Vehicle Design at the Royal College of Art in London, sponsored by Audi AG, where he earned an MA in 1990. The same year, he began his career in the interior design department of Audi Design in Ingolstadt. He transferred to the Audi Design Center in Munich in 1993, and in 1995 he was entrusted with the planning and set-up of the Design Center Europe in Sitges, Spain. Sielaff returned to Ingolstadt in 1997 as Head of Audi Interior Design. In 2002, he contributed to the development and strategic orientation of the design concept for the Audi brand group. Sielaff left Audi in 2003 to join Daimler Chrysler where, as Design Director of the Interior Competence Center in Sindelfingen, he was responsible for the interior design of all current models. He has been Head of Audi Design in Ingolstadt since March 2006.

RUPERT STADLER is Chairman of the Board of Management of Audi AG and Member of the Board of Volkswagen AG. He studied Business Management at Augsburg University of Applied Sciences, with an emphasis on Corporate Planning/Controllership and Finance, Banking and Investment. Stadler began his career at Philips Kommunikation Industrie AG in Nuremberg before joining Audi AG in Ingolstadt in 1990, where he assumed various controlling tasks in the area of sales and marketing. He transferred to Volkswagen/Audi España SA in Barcelona as Commercial Director in 1994. From 1997, Stadler was Head of the Board of Management's Office for the Volkswagen Group, as well as Head of Group Product Planning. Stadler has been a Member of the Board of Audi AG since January 1, 2003. He was responsible for the Finance and Organizational Division from April 1, 2003 to August 31, 2007. On January 1, 2007 Rupert Stadler was named Chairman of the Board of Audi AG, and he was appointed to the Board of Volkswagen AG on January 1, 2010.

PUBLISHER'S INFORMATION

Publishing Company
Trademark Publishing, Westendstr. 87, 60325 Frankfurt am Main, Germany, www.trademarkpublishing.de

Editorial Team
Stylepark AG, Brönnerstraße 22, 60313 Frankfurt am Main, Germany, www.stylepark.com

Essays
Audi Think Tank, Claudia Beckmann, Aric Chen, Horant Fassbinder, Jörg Häntzschel, Sandra Hofmeister, Kent Martinussen, Christine Maukel, Vicky Richardson, Deyan Sudjic, Philip Ursprung, Thomas Wagner, Heinrich Wefing

Graphic design
Antonia Henschel, SIGN Kommunikation GmbH, Frankfurt am Main, Germany, www.sign.de

Production
Remo Weiss, SIGN Kommunikation GmbH, Frankfurt am Main, Germany, www.sign.de

Translations
Claudia Kotte, Berlin, Germany
Klaus Roth, Munich, Germany
Ingrid Weyher, Berlin, Germany

Proof reading
Dorle Ellmers, Frankfurt am Main, Germany
Barbara Schmidt-Runkel, Rottenburg, Germany
John Sykes, Cologne, Germany

Printed by
Universitätsdruckerei H. Schmidt, Mainz, Germany

ISBN 978-3-9813228-3-5

www.audi-urban-future-award.com

Audi
Urban Future
Award
Building
a Vision for
2030

Curated by **STYLEPARK**